THE
SET OF THE
SAIL

THE
SET OF THE
SAIL

A. W. TOZER

EDITED BY HARRY VERPLOEGH

FOREWORD BY R. T. KENDALL

STL Books

Bromley, Kent

Kingsway Publications

Eastbourne

Copyright © Christian Publications 1986

First published in the USA by Christian Publications,
3825 Hartzdale Drive, Camp Hill, PA 17011

First British edition 1987

Biblical quotations are from the
Authorised Version (crown copyright)

British Library Cataloguing in Publication Data

Tozer, A. W.
  The set of the sail.
  1. Christian life
  I. Title II. Verploegh, Harry
  248.4   BV4501.2

    STL   ISBN 1 85078 029 3
  Kingsway   ISBN 0 86065 604 7

STL Books are published by Send The Light
(Operation Mobilisation), PO Box 48, Bromley, Kent, England

Published jointly with Kingsway Publications Ltd,
Lottbridge Drove, Eastbourne, E. Sussex, BN23 6NT

Typesetting, production and printing in England by
Nuprint Ltd, Harpenden, Herts, AL5 4SE

Contents

Foreword

The name *A. W. Tozer* is probably better known in North America than in Britain, although there has been an increasing interest in him and his writings over here in recent years. The reason for this will become apparent by the quality of his thinking in these forty-four essays.

I myself do not recall reading Tozer until I came to Britain. And yet it was not his writings but tape recordings of his sermons that motivated me to read his books. A friend gave me a number of tapes by him when I was undergoing a severe trial several years ago. So moved was I by his preaching that I took five of his books with me on a week's holiday in Spain. I remember the impact of his thinking more than I do that week in the sun!

He is often spoken of as a prophet but it should be said that his role relates more to the superficiality of the modern Church than the the sinfulness of contemporary society. He did not suffer spiritual folly gladly!

Tozer's appeal to the serious Christian is his no-nonsense approach to faith and spirituality. He has an ingenious capacity to put his finger on 'what is wrong'; the reader is often left to think for himself as to 'what is right'. If we agree with his diagnosis, it does not take much wisdom to discover our next move—as he himself would put it.

Much of this volume is devoted to the matter of *thinking*. He eschews pietism, literalism and religious activity for their rivalry of, if not substitution for, discipleship. The heart of Tozer is perhaps best summed up in his statement: 'We cannot know God by thinking alone, but we can never know Him very well without a lot of hard thinking.'

Every Christian who has a desire to know God better will want to be acquainted with A. W. Tozer's writings, and I cannot imagine a better introduction to him than this volume of essays.

R. T. KENDALL
Westminster Chapel, London
July 1987

Editor's Introduction

This selection of hitherto uncollected editorials should be considered the seventh in a series. It follows six books—*The Root of the Righteous* (1955), *Born after Midnight* (1959), *Of God and Men* (1960), *That Incredible Christian* (1964), *Man, the Dwelling Place of God* (1966) and *God Tells the Man Who Cares* (1970). All seven consist of editorials written by A. W. Tozer while he served as editor of *The Alliance Witness* [1950–63], the official magazine of The Christian and Missionary Alliance.

The favourable reception given the essays in this book when they first appeared as editorials has led to their publication in this more permanent form. Like the others, these selections were born in the midst of life, in the rough seas where the children of God voyage. I read them when they first appeared, and in the rereading I still find them thought-provoking, challenging and helpful. They lead to a right relationship with God.

A. W. Tozer rarely leaves us in doubt as to how to position ourselves for spiritual development. 'We must,' he urges, 'set our sails in the will of God,' and then 'we will certainly find ourselves moving in the right direction, no matter which way the wind blows.'

HARRY VERPLOEGH
Wheaton, Illinios, USA
April 1986

1

The Set of the Sail

That religion lies in the will is an axiom of theology. Not how we feel but what we will determines our spiritual direction. An old poem states it for us:

One ship drives east and another drives west
With the selfsame winds that blow;
'Tis the set of the sails
And not the gales
Which tell us the way to go.

Ella Wheeler Wilcox

Though we do not hear much of it in this age of spineless religion, there is nevertheless much in the Bible about the place of moral determination in the service of the Lord. 'Jacob vowed a vow' – and it was the beginning of a very wonderful life with God. The following years brought a great many vicissitudes, and Jacob did not always acquit himself like a true man of God, but his early determination kept him on course, and he came through victorious at last.

Daniel 'purposed in his heart' – and God honoured his purpose. Jesus set His face like a flint and walked straight toward the cross. Paul 'determined not to know any thing among you, save Jesus Christ, and him crucified' – and in that determined spirit ignored the learned philosophers, preached a gospel that was accounted foolishness and earned himself a reputation for ignorance, though he was easily the greatest brain of his generation.

These are only a few of the many men and women of the Bible who have left us a record of spiritual greatness born out of a will firmly set to do the will of God. They did not try to float to heaven on a perfumed cloud, but cheerfully accepted the fact that 'with purpose of heart they must cleave unto the Lord'.

In the kingdom of God what we *will* is accepted as what we *are*. 'If any man will,' said our Lord, 'let him.' God does not desire to destroy our wills, but to sanctify them. In that terrible, wonderful moment of surrender it may be that we feel that our will has been broken for ever, but such is not the case. In His conquest of the soul God does not destroy any of its normal powers. He purges the will and brings it into union with His own, but He never breaks it.

In the diaries of some of God's greatest saints will be found vows and solemn pledges made in moments of great grace when the presence of God was so real and so wonderful that the reverent worshipper felt he dared to say anything, to make any promise, with the full assurance that God would enable him to carry out his holy intention. The self-confident and irresponsible boast of a Peter is one thing and is not to be confused with the hushed and trustful vow of a David or a Daniel. Neither should Peter's embarrassing debacle dissuade us from making vows of our own. The heart gives character to our pledges, and God knows the difference between an impulsive promise and a reverent declaration of intention.

Let us, then, set our sails in the will of God. If we do this we will certainly find ourselves moving in the right direction, no matter which way the wind blows.

2

The Power of Silence

There are truths that can never be learned except in the noise and confusion of the market-place or in the tough brutality of combat. The tumult and the shouting teach their own rough lessons. No man is quite a man who has not been to the school of work and war, who has not heard the cry at birth and the sigh at life's parting.

But there is another school where the soul must go to learn its best eternal lessons. It is the school of silence. 'Be still and know,' said the psalmist, and there is a profound philosophy there, of universal application.

Prayer among evangelical Christians is always in danger of degenerating into a glorified gold rush. Almost every book on prayer deals with the 'get' element mainly. How to get things we want from God occupies most of the space. Now, we gladly admit that we may ask for and receive specific gifts and benefits in answer to prayer, but we must never forget that the highest kind of prayer is never the making of requests. Prayer at its holiest moment is the entering into God to a place of such blessed union as makes miracles seem tame and remarkable answers to prayer appear something very far short of wonderful by comparison.

Holy men of soberer and quieter times than ours knew well the power of silence. David said, 'I was dumb with silence, I held my peace, even from good; and my sorrow was stirred. My heart was hot within me; while I was musing the fire burned: then spake I with my tongue.' There is a tip here for God's modern prophets. The heart seldom gets hot while the mouth is open. A closed mouth before God and a silent heart are indispensable for the reception of certain kinds of truth. No man is qualified to speak who has not first listened.

It might well be a wonderful revelation to some Christians if they were to get completely quiet for a short time, long enough, let us say, to get acquainted with their own souls, and to listen in the silence for the deep voice of the Eternal God. The experience, if repeated often enough, would do more to cure our ulcers than all the pills that ever rolled across a desk.

3

The Truth's Most Powerful Ally

The most effective argument for Christianity is still the good lives of those who profess it.

A company of pure-living and cheerful Christians in the community is a stronger proof that Christ is risen than any learned treatise could ever be. And a further advantage is that, while the average person could not be hired to read a theological work, no one can evade the practical argument presented by the presence of holy men and women.

To the sons and daughters of this tense and highly mechanised age a holy life may seem unpardonably dull and altogether lacking in interest, but among all the fancy, interest-catching toys of the world a holy life stands apart as the only thing slated to endure.

'The stars make no noise,' says the Italian proverb; yet they have outlived all man's civilisations and in their unassuming silence have shone on through the centuries, preaching their simple doctrine of God and enduring things. Francis of Assisi composed some sublime hymns and preached some quaint sermons, but for none of these is he known and by none of these has he captured the moral imagination of mankind. The utter purity of his life it is which has won him a lasting place in the hearts of every seeker after God.

When the Church in America rejected the example of good men and chose for her pattern the celebrity of the hour, she suffered a greater loss than she has since discovered. Human greatness cannot be determined by popularity polls nor by the number of lines any man rates in the public press. It is altogether unlikely that we know who our greatest men are. One thing is sure, however – the greatest man alive today is the best man alive today. That is not open to debate.

To discover the good great man (granted that it would be to our profit to do so) would require more than human wisdom. For the holy man is also the humble man and the humble man will not advertise himself nor allow others to do it for him. Spiritual virtues run deep and silent. Like the tide or the pull of gravitation or the shining of the sun, they work without noise, but their gracious ministrations are felt around the whole earth.

The Christian who is zealous to promote the cause of Christ can begin by living in the power of the Spirit and so reproducing the life of Christ in the sight of men. In deep humility and without ostentation he can let his light shine. The world may pretend not to see, but it will see, nevertheless, and more than likely it will get into serious trouble with its conscience over what it sees.

4

We Are Committed to the Whole Message

To many observing persons today it appears that conversion does not do for people as much as it once did. Too often the experience passes, leaving the seeker unsatisfied and deeply disappointed. Some who are thus affected, and who are too sincere to play with religion, walk out on the whole thing and turn back frankly to the old life. Others try to make what they can out of a bad bargain and gradually adjust themselves to a modified and imperfect form of Christianity spiced up with synthetic fun and enlivened by frequent shots of stimulants in the form of 'gimmicks', to give it relish and sparkle.

The knowledge that revival campaigns can come and go without raising the moral level of the cities and towns where they are held should surely give us serious pause. Something is wrong somewhere. Could it be that the cause behind this undeniable failure of the gospel to effect moral change is a further-back failure of the messenger to grasp the real meaning of his message? Could it be that, in his eagerness to gain one more convert, he makes the way of life too easy? It would seem so. In other times it was not an uncommon thing to witness the wholesale closing of saloons and brothels as a direct result of the preaching of the message of Christ in revival campaigns. Surely there must have been a difference of emphasis between the message they preached in those days and the ineffective message we preach today.

To allow the gospel only its etymological meaning of *good news* is to restrict it so radically as actually to make it something it is not. That 'Christ died for our sins according to the scriptures' is good news indeed. That He, 'having by himself purged our sins, sat down on the right hand of the Majesty' in the heavens from which exalted position He mediates grace to all believers, is wonderful, heartening news for the sin-burdened race. But to limit the Christian message to this one truth alone is to rob it of much of its meaning and create a bad misunderstanding among those who hear the resultant preaching.

The fact is that the New Testament message embraces a great deal more than an offer of free pardon. It is a message of pardon, and for that may God be praised; but it is also a message of repentance. It is a message of atonement, but it is also a message of temperance and righteousness and godliness in this present world. It tells us that we must accept a Saviour, but it tells us also that we must *deny* ungodliness and worldly lusts. The gospel message includes the idea of amendment, of separation from the world, of cross-carrying and loyalty to the kingdom of God even unto death.

To be strictly technical, these latter truths are corollaries of the gospel, and not the gospel itself; but they are part and parcel of the total message which we are commissioned to declare. No man has authority to divide the truth and preach only a part of it. To do so is to weaken it and render it without effect.

This is more than a mere splitting of definitions. It has

real consequences among Christian workers and, what is more serious, it has consequences among the trusting seekers who come to these workers for counsel. To offer a sinner the gift of salvation based upon the work of Christ, while at the same time allowing him to retain the idea that the gift carries with it no moral implications, is to do him untold injury where it hurts him worst.

Many evangelical teachers insist so strongly upon free, unconditional grace as to create the impression that sin is not a serious matter and that God cares very little about it. He is concerned only with our escaping the consequences. The gospel, then, in practical application means little more than a way to escape the fruits of our past. The heart that has felt the weight of its own sin and along with this has seen the dread whiteness of the Most High God will never believe that a message of forgiveness without transformation is a message of good news. To remit a man's past without transforming his present is to violate the moral sincerity of his own heart. To that kind of thing God will be no party.

We must have courage to preach the whole message. By so doing we shall undoubtedly lose a few friends and make a number of enemies. But the true Christian will not grieve too much about that. He has enough to do to please his Lord and Saviour and to be true to the souls of all men. That may well occupy him too completely to leave much time for regrets over the displeasure of misguided men.

5

'I Believe in the Communion of Saints'

Without doubt the most important body on earth is the Church of God which He purchased with His own blood.

Unfortunately the word 'church' itself has taken on meanings which it did not originally have and has suffered untold injury in the house both of its enemies and of its friends.

The meaning of the word for the true Christian was fixed by our Lord and His apostles. What they meant by it is what we must mean by it; and no man and no angel has authority to change it.

The simple etymological meaning is easy to discover, but its larger significance must be learned from the New Testament scriptures. All that is meant by that wondrous word cannot be stated in one sentence, nor in one paragraph, nor scarcely in one book.

The universal Church is the body of Christ, the bride of the Lamb, the habitation of God through the Spirit, the pillar and ground of the truth.

The local church is a community of ransomed men, a minority group, a colony of heavenly souls dwelling apart on the earth, a division of soldiers on a foreign soil, a band of reapers, working under the direction of the

Lord of the harvest, a flock of sheep following the Good Shepherd, a brotherhood of like-minded men, a visible representative of the Invisible God.

It is most undesirable to conceive of our churches as 'Works', or 'Projects'. If such words must be used, then let them be understood as referring to the earthly and legal aspect of things only. A true church is something supernatural and divine, and is in direct lineal descent from that first church at Jerusalem. Insofar as it is a church, it is spiritual; its social aspect is secondary and may be imitated by any group regardless of its religious qualities or lack of them. The spiritual essence of a true church cannot be reproduced anywhere but in a company of renewed and inwardly united believers.

The Christian life begins with the individual; a soul has a saving encounter with God and the new life is born. Not all the pooled efforts of any church can make a Christian out of a lost man. But once the 'great transaction's done' the communion of believers will be found to be the best environment for the new life. Men are made for each other, and this is never more apparent than in the church.

All else being equal, the individual Christian will find in the communion of a local church the most perfect atmosphere for the fullest development of his spiritual life. There also he will find the best arena for the largest exercise of those gifts and powers with which God may have endowed him.

The religious solitary may gain on a few points, and he may escape some of the irritations of the crowd, but he is a half-man, nevertheless, and worse, he is a half-Christian. Every solitary experience, if we would realise its beneficial effects, should be followed immediately by a return to our own company. There will be found the faith of Christ in its most perfect present manifestation.

But one thing must be kept in mind: these things are

true only where the local church is a church indeed, where the communion of saints is more than a phrase from the Creed but is realised and practiced in faith and love. Those religio-social institutions, with which we are all too familiar, where worship is a form, the sermon an essay and the prayer an embarrassed address to someone who isn't there, certainly do not qualify as churches under any scriptural terms with which we are acquainted.

The elements of a true church are few and easy to possess. They are a company of believers, the Lord, the Spirit and the Word of the Living God. Let the Lord be worshipped, the Spirit be obeyed, the Word be expounded and followed as the only rule for faith and conduct, and the power of God will begin to show itself as it did to Samson in the camp of Dan.

The church will produce a spiritual culture all its own, wholly unlike anything created by the mind of man and superior to any culture known on earth, ancient or modern. God is getting His people ready for another world, and He uses the local church as a workshop in which to carry on His blessed work.

That Christian is a happy one who has found a company of true believers in whose heavenly fellowship he can live and love and labour. And nothing else on earth should be as dear to him nor command from him such a degree of loyalty and devotion.

6

We Must Try the Spirits

These are times of moral and religious confusion and it is sometimes hard to distinguish the false from the true.

Our faithful Lord has tried to save us from the consequences of our own blindness by repeated warnings and many careful instructions. It will pay us to give close attention to His words.

Toward the end of the age, we are told, there shall be a time of stepped-up religious activity and frenzied expectation, growing out of the turbulent conditions prevailing among nations. The language is familiar to most Christians: 'Wars and rumours of wars...nation shall rise against nation...famines, and pestilences, and earthquakes, in divers places.... Then shall they deliver you up to be afflicted, and shall kill you: and ye shall be hated of all nations...and then shall many be offended, and shall betray one another, and shall hate one another.'

Concurrent with this state of affairs will be a great increase in religious excitement and supernatural happenings generally. 'For many shall come in my name, saying, I am Christ; and shall deceive many.... And many false prophets shall rise.... Then if any man shall say unto you, Lo, here is Christ, or there; believe it not. For there shall arise false Christs, and false prophets, and shall show great signs and wonders; insomuch that, if it were possible, they shall deceive the very elect.'

Many tender-minded Christians fear to sin against love by daring to inquire into anything that comes wearing the cloak of Christianity and breathing the name of Jesus. They dare not examine the credentials of the latest prophet to hit their town lest they be guilty of rejecting something which may be of God. They timidly remember how the Pharisees refused to accept Christ when He came, and they do not want to be caught in the same snare, so they either reserve judgement or shut their eyes and accept everything without question. This is supposed to indicate a high degree of spirituality. But in sober fact it indicates no such thing. It may indeed be evidence of the absence of the Holy Spirit.

Gullibility is not synonymous with spirituality. Faith is not a mental habit leading its possessor to open his mouth and swallow everything that has about it the colour of the supernatural. Faith keeps its heart open to whatever is of God, and rejects everything that is not of God, however wonderful it may be.

'Try the spirits' is a command of the Holy Spirit to the Church. We may sin as certainly by approving the spurious as by rejecting the genuine. And the current habit of refusing to take sides is not the way to avoid the question. To appraise things with a heart of love and then to act on the results is an obligation resting upon every Christian in the world. And the more as we see the day approaching.

How can we tell whether or not a man or a religious demonstration is of God? The answer is easy to find, but it will take courage to follow the facts as God reveals them to us.

The tests for spiritual genuineness are two: First, the leader must be a good man and full of the Holy Ghost. Christianity is nothing if not moral. No tricks of theology, no demonstrations of supernatural wonders, no evidences of blind devotion on the part of the public can decide whether or not God is in the man or the movement. Every servant of Christ must be pure of heart and holy of life. While sinless perfection is not likely to be found among even the best of men, still the leader to be trusted is the one who lives as nearly like Christ as possible and who knows how to repent in sorrow of heart when he sins against his Lord by any act or word. The man God honours will be humble, self-effacing, self-sacrificing, modest, clean-living, free from the love of money, eager to promote the honour of God and just as eager to disclaim any credit or praise on his own part. His financial accounts will bear inspection, his ethical standards will be high and his personal life above reproach.

But the test of moral goodness is not enough. Every man must submit his work to the scriptural test. It is not enough that he be able to quote from the Bible at great length or that he claim for himself great and startling experiences with God. Go back to the law and to the testimony. If he speak not according to the Word it is because there is no light in him. We who are invited to follow him have every right, as well as a solemn obligation, to test his work according to the Word of God. We must demand that every claimant for our confidence present a clean bill of health from the Holy Scriptures; that he do more than weave in a text occasionally, or hold up the Bible dramatically before the eyes of his hearers. His doctrines must be those of the Scriptures. The Bible must dominate his preaching. He must preach according to the Word of God.

The price of following a false guide on the desert may

be death. The price of heeding wrong advice in business may be bankruptcy. The price of trusting to a quack doctor may be permanent loss of health. The price of putting confidence in a pseudo-prophet may be moral and spiritual tragedy. Let us take heed that no man deceive us.

AMEN

7

Facing Both Ways

Like a doctor with a sick patient whose disease eludes diagnosis, religious leaders have for some years been aware that there is something seriously wrong with evangelicalism and have yet been unable to lay their finger upon the precise trouble. The symptoms they have discovered in abundance, but the cause behind them has been hard to locate. Mostly we have spent our time correcting symptoms, having all the while an uneasy feeling that our remedies did not go deep enough.

One odd mark of the disease of which we speak is an impulse on the part of the patient to jump up and down and shout that he never felt better in his life. Yet if the New Testament and the example of eminent saints represent a normal state of spiritual health, our patient is not only below standard but actually gravely ill.

Knowing that a disease that cannot be identified invariably calls out a flock of untrained experts to analyse and prescribe, we yet risk a pronouncement upon the condition of evangelical Christianity in our day and we believe we may not be too far from the truth.

The trouble seems to be a disorder of the spiritual nerve system which we might, for the lack of a proper term, call dual orientation. Its dominant characteristic appears to be crossed wires among the nerve ganglia of the soul resulting in an inability to control the direction of the life. The patient starts one direction and before he knows it he is going another. His inward eyes do not coordinate; each one sees a different object and seeks to lead the steps toward it. The individual is caught in the middle, trying to be true to both foci of the heart, and never knowing which he would rather follow. Evangelicalism (at least in many circles) is suffering from this strange division of life-purpose. Its theology faces toward the East and the sacred temple of Jehovah. Its active interests face toward the world and the temple of Dagon. Doctrinally it is Christian, but actually it is a pagan mentality, pagan scale of values and pagan religious principles.

Let a man but become, as the early Methodists would have said, 'soundly converted', and certain things will begin to happen in his life. He will experience a wonderful unification of personality and a turning about of the whole life toward God and heavenly things. Though he will undoubtedly suffer from the inward struggle described in the seventh chapter of Romans, yet his direction will be established beyond any doubt and his face will remain turned toward the City of God.

That word 'direction' should have more emphasis these days, for the most important thing about a life is its direction. David hardly said anything more significant than this: 'I have set the Lord always before me: because he is at my right hand, I shall not be moved.' And the Hebrews' writer summed it all up in one sentence, 'Looking unto Jesus, the author and finisher of our faith.'

An emotional conversion which stops short of Christ-orientation is inadequate for life and death, and, unless new help comes from some quarter, it may easily be worse than no religious experience at all. And just this would appear to be the source of our bad orientation. The original experience of conversion was not sufficiently radical to turn the life wholly to God and things eternal. Then when religious leaders found that they had on their hands half-converted persons who wanted to be saved but would not turn fully to God, they tried to meet the situation by providing a twilight-zone religion which did not demand too much and which did offer something. Better have them halfway in, they reasoned, than all the way out. We know now how bad that reasoning was.

With large blocks of evangelicals praying and preaching like Christians while they live and talk like worldlings, how much longer may we expect them to remain evangelical? Apostasy always begins with the conduct. First there is a wrong orientation of the life, a facing toward the lost world with yearning and enjoyment; later there comes a gradual surrender of the truth itself and a slipping back into unbelief. That has happened to individuals and denominations and it can happen to the whole present evangelical communion if it is not checked before it is too late.

For this cause, the facing-both-ways attitude of our present Christianity is something to be alarmed about. And if that attitude were the result of plain backsliding there would be much more reason for optimism. Un-christian acts done by a Christian through weakness and over the protests of his better heart may be bad enough, but they are not likely to be fatal. But when he does them with the sanction of his teachers and with the belief that they are all a part of the Christian way, how is he to be rescued?

8

What Profit in Prayer?

The skeptic in the book of Job asked the disdainful question, 'What is the Almighty, that we should serve him, and what profit should we have, if we pray unto him?'

The whole tone of the remark shows that it is meant to be rhetorical. The doubter, believing the question could have no answer, tossed it off contemptuously and turned away, like Pilate, without waiting for a reply. But we have an answer. God Himself has supplied it, and the universal consensus of the ages has added an 'Amen'.

In the eleventh chapter of Hebrews we have a long list of benefits which faith brings to its possessors: justification, deliverance, fruitfulness, endurance, victory over enemies, courage, strength and even resurrection from the dead. And everything that is attributed to faith might with equal truth be attributed to prayer, for faith and true prayer are like two sides of the same coin. They are inseparable.

Men may, and often do, pray without faith (though this is not true prayer), but it is unthinkable that men should have faith and not pray. The biblical formula is the 'prayer of faith'. Prayer and faith are here bound together by the little preposition 'of', and 'what God hath joined together, let not man put assunder'. Faith is only genuine as it eventuates into prayer.

When Tennyson wrote 'More things are wrought by prayer than this world dreams of', he probably uttered a truth of vaster significance than even he understood. While it is not always possible to trace an act of God to its prayer-cause, it is yet safe to say that prayer is behind everything that God does for the sons of men here upon earth. One would gather as much from a simple reading of the Scriptures.

What profit is there in prayer? 'Much every way.' Whatever God can do faith can do, and whatever faith can do prayer can do when it is offered in faith. An invitation to prayer is, therefore, an invitation to Omnipotence, for prayer engages the Omnipotent God and brings Him into our human affairs. Nothing is impossible to the man who prays in faith, just as nothing is impossible with God. This generation has yet to prove all that prayer can do for believing men and women.

It was a saying of George Müller that faith grows with use. If we would have great faith we must begin to use the little faith we already have. Put it to work by reverent and faithful praying, and it will grow and become stronger day by day. Dare today to trust God for something small and ordinary and next week or next year you may be able to trust Him for answers bordering on the miraculous. Everyone has some faith, said Müller; the difference among us is one of degree only, and the man of small faith may be simply the one who has not dared to exercise the little faith he has.

According to the Bible, we have because we ask, or we have not because we ask not. It does not take much wisdom to discover our next move. Is it not to pray, and pray again and again till the answer comes? God waits to be invited to display His power in behalf of His people.

The world situation is such that nothing less than God can straighten it out. Let us not fail the world and disappoint God by failing to pray.

9

The True Saint is Different

The church's mightiest influence is felt when she is different from the world in which she lives. Her power lies in her being different, rises with the degree in which she differs and sinks as the difference diminishes.

This is so fully and clearly taught in the Scriptures and so well illustrated in Church history that it is hard to see how we can miss it. But miss it we do, for we hear constantly that the Church must try to be as much like the world as possible, excepting, of course, where the world is too, too sinful; and we are told to get adjusted to the world and 'be all things to all men'. (This use of the passage, incidentally, illustrates Peter's saying that 'Our beloved brother Paul' wrote some things which the unlearned and the unstable wrest to their own destruction.)

One sure mark of the Church's heavenly character is that she is different from the rest of mankind; similarity is a mark of her fall. The sons of God and the sons of men are morally and spiritually separated, and between them there is a great gulf fixed. When religious persons try to bridge that gulf by compromise they violate the very principles of the kingdom of God.

Men are impressed with the message of the Church just as far and as long as she is different from themselves.

When she seeks to be like them they no longer respect her. They believe (and rightly) that she is playing false to herself and to them. The moral jar that results when an indoctrinated son of Adam meets a son of heaven is one of the most wholesome things that can happen to both of them. And contrary to common opinion, men are more inclined to follow the way of Christ when they are compelled to make a radical alteration in their lives than they are when the way is made easy for them. The human heart senses its need to be changed, and when religion appears offering life without such change, it is not taken seriously by thinking men. The superficial, the insincere, may embrace such a low-powered brand of religion, but the seeking heart must reject it as false and unreal.

All conformity to the world is a negation of our Christian character and a surrender of our heavenly position.

Let us plant ourselves on the hill of Zion and invite the world to come over to us, but never under any circumstances will we go over to them. The cross is the symbol of Christianity, and the cross speaks of death and separation, never of compromise. No one ever compromised with a cross. The cross separated between the dead and the living. The timid and the fearful will cry 'Extreme!' and they will be right. The cross is the essence of all that is extreme and final. The message of Christ is a call across a gulf from death to life, from sin to righteousness and from Satan to God.

The first step for any Christian who is seeking spiritual power is to accept his unique position as a son of heaven temporarily detained on the earth, and to begin to live as becometh a saint. The sharp line of demarcation between him and the world will appear at once – and the world will never quite forgive him. And the sons of earth will make him pay well for separation, but it is a price he will gladly pay for the privilege of walking in fruitfulness and power.

10

Faith Rests upon God's Character

All things else being equal, the destiny of a man or nation may safely be predicted from the idea of God which that man or that nation holds. No nation can rise higher than its conception of God. While Rome held to her faith in the stern old gods of the Pantheon she remained an iron kingdom. Her citizens unconsciously imitated the character of her gods, however erroneous their conception of the Deity might have been. When Rome began to think loosely about God she began to rot inwardly, and that rot never stopped till it brought her to the ground. So it must always be with men and nations.

A church is strong or weak just as it holds to a high or low idea of God. For faith rests not primarily upon promises, but upon character. A believer's faith can never rise higher than his conception of God. A promise is never better or worse than the character of the one who makes it. An inadequate conception of God must result in a weak faith, for faith depends upon the character of God just as a building rests upon its foundation.

This explains why unbelief is such a grievous sin; it is pure libel against the Lord of heaven and earth.

Unbelief judges God to be unworthy of confidence and withholds its trust from Him. Can there be a more heinous sin than this? 'He that believeth not God hath made him a liar' (1 John 5:10). Our hearts shrink from the full implications of such a statement, but would not this seem to teach that unbelief attributes to God the character of Satan? Jesus said of Satan, 'He is a liar and the father of it.' Unbelief says virtually the same thing of God.

How then shall unbelief be cured and faith be strengthened? Surely not by straining to believe the Scriptures, as some do. Not by a frantic effort to believe the promises of God. Not by gritting our teeth and determining to exercise faith by an act of the will. All this has been tried – and it never helps. To try thus to super-induce faith is to violate the laws of the mind and to do violence to the simple psychology of the heart.

What is the answer? Job told us, 'Acquaint thyself with him and be at peace,' and Paul said, 'So then faith cometh by hearing, and hearing by the word of God.' These two verses show the way to a strong and lasting faith: *Get acquainted with God through reading the Scriptures, and faith will come naturally.* This presupposes that we come to the Scriptures humbly, repudiating self-confidence and opening our minds to the sweet operations of the Spirit.

Otherwise stated: Faith comes effortlessly to the heart as we elevate our conceptions of God by a prayerful digestion of His Word. And such faith endures, for it is grounded upon the rock.

11

Salvation Walks the Earth

Matthew 16:24 *If any man will come after me, let him deny himself, and take up his cross, and follow me.*

It is like the Lord to fasten a world upon nothing, and make it stay in place. Here He takes that wonderful, mysterious microcosm we call the human soul and makes its future weal or woe to rest upon a single word – 'if'. 'If any man,' He says, and teaches at once the universal inclusiveness of His invitation, and the freedom of the human will. Everyone may come; no one need come, and whoever does come, comes because he chooses to.

Every man holds his future in his hand. Not the dominant world leader only, but the inarticulate man lost in anonymity is a 'man of destiny'. He decides which way his soul shall go. He chooses, and destiny waits on the nod of his head. He decides, and hell enlarges herself, or heaven prepares another mansion. So much of Himself has God given to men.

There is a strange beauty in the ways of God with men. He sends salvation to the world in the person of a man and sends that man to walk the busy ways saying, 'If any man will come after me.' No drama, no fanfare, no tramp of marching feet or tumult of shouting. A kindly stranger walks through the earth and so quiet is His voice that it is sometimes lost in the hurly-burly; but it is the last voice of God, and until we become quiet to hear it we have no authentic message. He bears good tidings from afar but He compels no man to listen. 'If any man will,' He says, and passes on. Friendly, courteous, unobtrusive, He yet bears the signet of the King. His word is divine authority, His eyes a tribunal, His face a Last Judgement.

'If any man will..., let him follow me,' He says, and some will rise and go after Him, but others give no heed to His voice. So the gulf opens between man and man, between those who will and those who will not. Silently, terribly the work goes on, as each one decides whether he will hear or ignore the voice of invitation. Unknown to the world, perhaps unknown even to the individual, the work of separation takes place. Each hearer of the voice must decide for himself, and he must decide on the basis of the evidence the message affords. There will be no thunder sound, no heavenly sign or light from heaven. The man is His own proof. The marks in His hand and feet are the insignia of His rank and office. He will not put Himself again on trial; He will not argue, but the morning of the Judgement will confirm what men in the twilight have decided.

And those who would follow Him must accept His conditions. 'Let him,' He says, and there is no appeal from His words. He will use no coercion, but neither will He compromise. Men cannot make the terms; they merely agree to them. Thousands turn from Him because they will not meet His conditions. He watches them as they go, for He loves them, but He will make no concessions. Admit one soul into the kingdom by compromise and that kingdom is no longer secure. Christ will be Lord, or He will be Judge. Every man must decide whether he will take Him as Lord now or face Him as Judge then.

What are the terms of discipleship? Only one with a perfect knowledge of mankind could have dared to make them. Only the Lord of men could have risked the effect of such rigorous demands: 'Let him deny himself.' We hear these words and shake our heads in astonishment. Can we have heard aright? Can the Lord lay down such severe rules at the door of the kingdom? He can and He does. If He is to save the man, He must save him from himself. It is the 'himself' which has enslaved and corrupted the man. Deliverance comes only by denial of that self. No man in his own strength can shed the chains with which self has bound him, but in the next breath the Lord reveals the source of the power which is to set the soul free: 'Let him take up his cross.' The cross has gathered in the course of the years much of beauty and symbolism, but the cross of which Jesus spoke had nothing of beauty in it. It was an instrument of death. Slaying men was its only function. Men did not wear that cross; but that cross wore men. It stood naked until a man was pinned on it, a living man fastened like some grotesque tie-pin on its breast to writhe and groan till death stilled and silenced him. That is the cross. Nothing less. And when it is robbed of its tears and blood and pain it is the cross no longer. 'Let him take... his cross,' said Jesus, and in death he will know deliverance from himself.

A strange thing under the sun is cross-less Christianity. The cross of Christendom is a no-cross, an ecclesiastical symbol. The cross of Christ is a place of death. Let each one be careful which cross he carries.

'And follow me.' Now the glory begins to break in upon the soul that has just returned from Calvary. 'Follow me' is an invitation, and a challenge, and a promise. The cross has been the end of a life and the beginning of a life. The life that ended there was a life of sin and slavery; the life that began there is a life of holiness and spiritual freedom. 'And follow me,' He says, and faith runs on tiptoe to keep pace with the advancing light. Until we know the programme of our risen Lord for all the years to come we can never know everything He meant when He invited us to follow Him. Each heart can have its own dream of fair worlds and new revelations, of the odyssey of the ransomed soul in the ages to come, but whoever follows Jesus will find at last that He has made the reality to outrun the dream.

12

God's Love and Ours

God being who and what He is must love Himself with pure and perfect love.

The persons of the Godhead love each other with a love so fiery, so tender, that it is all a burning flame of intense desire ineffable.

God is Himself the only being whom He can love directly; all else that He loves is for His own sake and because He finds some reflection of Himself there.

God loves His mute creation because He sees in it an imperfect representation of His own wisdom and power. He loves the angels and seraphim because He sees in them some likeness of His holiness. He loves men because He beholds in them a fallen relic of His own image.

Potentially God loves all men alike, but His active love lights upon some men more than upon others, the degree depending upon how much of Himself He is able to impart to them. The truly Christlike soul enjoys more of God's love because God sees in it a truer image of Himself than in a soul less purified. God loves His Son with infinite perfection because He is 'the brightness of his glory, and the express image of his person'.

God desires that all men should become Christlike, for in so doing they present larger and more perfect objects for the reception of His outpoured love.

Conformity to the nature of Christ on the part of a redeemed man restores the image of God in the soul and thus makes it possible for God to lavish on the soul without restraint all the boundless love of which He is the original fountain.

It is hard for a sinful man to believe that God loves Him. His own accusing conscience tells him it could not be so. He knows that he is an enemy of God and alienated in his mind through wicked works, and he sees in himself a thousand moral discrepancies that unfit him for the just enjoyment of so pure a love. Yet the whole Bible proclaims the love of God for sinful men. We must believe in His love because He declares it and avail ourselves of the sanctifying grace of Christ in order to receive and enjoy that love to the full.

'For our soul is so specially loved of Him that is highest, that it overpasseth the knowing of all creatures ... there is no creature that is made that may fully know how much and how sweetly and how tenderly our Maker loveth us. And therefore we may with grace and His help (behold) with everlasting marvel this high, overpassing, inestimable love that Almighty God hath to us of His goodness. And therefore we may ask of our Lover with reverence all that we will.'

God is love, and is for that reason the source of all the love there is. He has set as the first of all commandments that we love Him with all our hearts, but He knows that the desired love can never originate with us. 'We love him, because he first loved us,' is the scriptural and psychological pattern. We can love Him as we ought only as He inflames our minds with holy desire.

Yet there is also a love of willing as well as of feeling. Though we may not be conscious of any great degree of inward sensation, we may set our wills to love God and the feeling will come of itself. Let us bring ourselves under obedience to His revealed Word and our love for Him will grow. Obedience will strengthen faith and faith will increase knowledge. And it is a well-known law of the spiritual life that our love for God will spring up and flourish just as our knowledge of Him increases. To know Him is to love Him, and to know Him better is to love Him more.

13

The Lord Giveth Knowledge

Elsewhere I have said that we cannot know God by thinking but that we must do a lot of thinking if we would know Him well. This sounds self-contradictory, but I am sure that the two statements are in full accord with each other.

The inability of the human mind to know God in a true and final sense is taken for granted throughout the Bible and even taught in plain words in such passages as these: 'No man knoweth the Son, but the Father; neither knoweth any man the Father, save the Son, and he to whomsoever the Son will reveal him.' 'The world by wisdom knew not God.' 'The things of God knoweth no man, but the Spirit of God.' God's nature is of another kind from anything with which the mind is acquainted; hence when the mind attempts to find out God it is confronted by obscurity. It is surrounded with mystery and blinded by the light no man can approach unto.

A consideration of this truth led some thinkers of the past to conclude that since it is impossible for man to discover God by means of any faculties he possesses, God must therefore remain not only unknown but unknowable. What these men overlooked was that when

God desires He can and does reveal Himself to men. The Spirit of God is able to make the spirit of man know and experience the awful mystery of God's essential being. It should be noted that the Spirit reveals God to the spirit of man, not to his intellect merely. The intellect can know God's attributes because these constitute that body of truth that can be known *about* God. The knowledge *of* God is for the spirit alone. Such knowledge comes not by intellection but by intuition.

To know God in the scriptural meaning of the term is to enter into experience of Him. It never means to know about. It is not a knowledge mediated by the intellect, but an unmediated awareness experienced by the soul on a plane too high for the mind to reach.

Where then is the place of the intellect in Christian experience? And why waste time thinking when we know beforehand that thought cannot bring us to the knowledge that is most of all to be desired, the knowledge of God? The answer is that the whole biblical revelation is addressed to the intellect and through the intellect reaches the will, the seat of the moral life; if the will responds in repentance and obedience, the Holy Spirit illuminates the penitent heart and reveals Christ, the image of God, to it. What began as an appeal to reason (Isaiah 1:18) ends in a spiritual experience wholly above reason.

God is concerned with the whole man and has designed that Christian experience should embrace the entire personality. The Christian faith deals not with the spiritual only but with the moral and the rational as well. The rational and moral elements in religion are the proper objects of thought and willingly yield their rich treasures to prayerful meditation. The Christian faith deals with God and man and what can be known about them and their relation one to the other. It contemplates creation, redemption, righteousness, sacred history, the destiny of mankind and the future of the world. Such truths, once they have been revealed by divine inspiration, lie where they can be got at by the redeemed intellect and wait to be exploited by the sons of the kingdom.

Under the illumination and guidance of the Holy Spirit the prayerful, studious believer can become a Christian philosopher, a sage, a doctor of divine things. More than that, he can become a man of God and a light to his generation.

I repeat, we cannot know God by thinking alone, but we can never know Him very well without a lot of hard thinking.

14

The Urge to Share

Spiritual experiences must be shared. It is not possible for very long to enjoy them alone. The very attempt to do so will destroy them.

The reason for this is obvious. The nearer our souls draw to God the larger our love will grow, and the greater our love the more unselfish we shall become and the greater our care for the souls of others. Hence increased spiritual experience, so far as it is genuine, brings with it a strong desire that others may know the same grace that we ourselves enjoy. This leads quite naturally to an increased effort to lead others to a closer and more satisfying fellowship with God.

The human race is one. God 'made of one blood all nations of men for to dwell on all the face of the earth', and He made the individual members of society for each other. Not the hermit but the man in the midst of society is in the place best to fulfill the purpose for which he was created. There may be circumstances when for a time it will be necessary for the seeker after God to wrestle alone like Jacob on the bank of the river, but the result of his lonely experience is sure to flow out to family and friend, and on out to society at last. In the nature of things it must be so.

The impulse to share, to impart, normally accompanies any true encounter with God and spiritual things. The woman at the well, after her soul-inspiring meeting with Jesus, left her waterpots, hurried into the city and tried to persuade her friends to come out and meet Him. 'Come, see a man,' she said, 'which told me all things that ever I did: is not this the Christ?' Her spiritual excitement could not be contained within her own heart. She had to tell someone.

Is it not possible that our Lord had this in mind when He spoke about the impossibility of secret discipleship? Have we misunderstood the true relationship between faith and testimony? Christ made it clear that there could be no such thing as secret discipleship and Paul said, 'With the heart man believeth unto righteousness; and with the mouth confession is made unto salvation.' This is usually understood to mean that God has laid upon us an arbitrary requirement to open our mouth in confession before salvation can become effective within us. Maybe that is the correct meaning of these verses. Or could it be that the confession is an *evidence* of the salvation which has come by faith to the heart, and where there is no impulse to impart, no outrushing of words in joyous testimony, there has been no true inward experience of saving grace?

The irrepressible urge to share spiritual blessings can explain a great many religious phenomena. It even goes so far as to create a kind of vicarious transfer of interest from one person to another, so that the blessed soul would if necessary give up its own blessing that another might receive. Only thus can that prayer of Moses be understood, 'Oh, this people have sinned a great sin, and have made them gods of gold. Yet now, if thou wilt forgive their sin – ; and if not, blot me, I pray thee, out of thy book which thou hast written' (Exodus 32:31, 32). His great care for Israel had made him incautious, almost rash, before the Lord in their behalf. Moses felt that for Israel to be forgiven was reward enough for him. This impulsive uprush of vicarious love can hardly be defended before the bar of pure reason. But God understood and complied with Moses' request.

The intense urge to have others enjoy the same spiritual privileges as himself once led Paul to make a statement so extreme, so reckless, that reason cannot approve it; only love can understand: 'I say the truth in Christ, I lie not, my conscience also bearing me witness in the Holy Ghost, that I have great heaviness and continual sorrow in my heart. For I could wish that myself were accursed from Christ for my brethren, my kinsmen according to the flesh' (Romans 9:1–3).

In the light of this it is quite easy to understand why all great Christian teachers have insisted that true spiritual experience must be shared. The careless person who remarks that he does not need to go to church to serve God is far from understanding the most elementary spiritual truths. By cutting himself off from the religious community he proves that he has never felt the deep urge to share – and for the very reason that he has nothing to share. He has never felt the constraining love of Christ, so he can go his way in silence. His withdrawal from the believing fellowship tells us more about him than he knows about himself.

'Being let go, they went to their own company.' So it was in the early Church and so it has always been when men meet God in saving encounter. They want to share the blessed benefits.

15

Dedication to What?

It is one of the ironies of modern life that after a word has been dropped from the Christian vocabulary because it no longer expresses any vital content in current church religion, it is often taken up by the world and made to mean not the same thing but something close to what it once meant in its original Christian usage.

Such a word is 'dedicate'. This word in its various forms was once used to express a sacred idea deriving straight from the Scriptures. Though the exact English word is not found in our Authorised Version, the idea runs from Genesis to Revelation and all through Jewish and Christian history.

A noticeable change has come over the word in recent years, a semantic degeneration that has secularised it almost completely, and oddly enough the dictionary definitions unwittingly follow the word down: '*Dedicate*. 1. To devote to the service of worship of a divine being. 2. To set apart to a definite use or service. 3. To inscribe by way of compliment as a book.' That is the way a late dictionary puts it, and in so doing furnishes its own spiritual commentary.

Now I have no quarrel with mere words. Whatever

current usage and an up-to-date dictionary declare a word to mean, that is what it means, whatever it may have meant before. But I am concerned when men mistake earth for heaven, confuse this world with the world to come and borrow sacred words to describe secular things – without knowing what they have done. That is precisely what has happened to the word *dedication*. Through a radical change of meaning it has been lost to the language of worship. And it is highly significant that up to this moment Christians have not felt sufficient inward pressure to create a new word that would mean what the old word once meant. Apparently not only the word is gone from us but the idea as well.

One reason for this is the current imperfect understanding of the Christian message. Scarcely anyone catches the imperious note in Christ's words. The Christian message has ceased to be a pronouncement and has become a proposition. Its invitational element has been pressed far out of proportion in the total scriptural scheme. Christ with His lantern, His apologetic stance and His weak pleading face has taken the place of the true Son of man whom John saw clothed with a garment down to the foot, girt with a golden girdle, whose head and hair are white like wool, whose eyes are as a flame of fire, whose feet are like burnished brass and whose voice is as the sound of many waters. The Christ of the tentative smile and air of puzzlement is not the Christ of God. The artists have been guilty of inadvertent idolatry in presenting to the world a false image of Christ. Only the Holy Spirit can reveal our Lord as He really is, and He does not paint in oils. He manifests Christ to the human spirit, not to our physical eyes.

Any public figure who is honest and who takes his job seriously is sure to be called a 'dedicated man' by some reporter or news commentator. The word is even used to describe persons deeply concerned about wildlife refuges or the conservation of natural resources. It is also applied to baseball players and stock car racers, and not long ago a young bullfighter enthusiast spoke to me in defence of that gory and perilous sport. He explained simply that the Spanish matador risks his life in the bullring 'because he is a dedicated man. The people want the thrill of seeing the bull killed and he puts his life in jeopardy to furnish that thrill for them.'

The 'dedicated' matador would likely win some sort of prize for sheer absurdity and may be allowed to stand as the uncrowned champion of all those who seek to waste their lives in the most foolish way. But dedication to vanity is not confined to bullfighters. The truth is, dedication of the life to anything or anyone short of God Himself, is a prostitution of noble powers and must bring a harvest of grief and disappointment at last. Only God is worthy of the soul He has made in His own image. To devote our lives to any cause, however worthy, is to sell ourselves short. Not money, position, fame, can justly claim our devotion. Art, literature, music also fall short. And, if God is forgotten, even the loftiest and most unselfish task is unworthy of the soul's full surrender. Complete dedication unto death in the cause of freedom, for instance, is a touching thing and has given to history many of her greatest heroes, but only the God of freedom should have our 'last full measure of devotion'.

These are strenuous times and men are being recruited everywhere to devote themselves to one or another master. Let us be careful. No one has any true right to claim my life except the one who gave His own life for my redemption. If He gets my full dedication then I may engage in any good and worthy cause under His Spirit's guidance. But anything short of complete devotion to Christ is inadequate and must end in futility and loss.

16

The Making of a Man

Though human nature as we know it now is fallen and morally degenerate, it yet stands at the top in the order of God's creation. Of no other being was it said, 'In the image of God created he him.'

Man's nature indicates that he was created for three things: To think, to worship and to work.

Under *think* may be included everything that the intellect can do, from the simplest act to the creation of an oratorio or the founding of an empire. In his ability to observe, to inquire, to collect data and to reason from it to causes, laws and principles, man stands easily supreme above all other creatures. The domestication of the wild forces of nature, the conquest of disease, the amelioration of the pains and woes of our physical organism – all has been done by the thinking man riding on the wings of his imagination out into the unknown and daring to entertain notions no one had entertained before.

To make out of the raw material that is a man a thinking man, an imaginative, dreaming man, is one of the most urgent tasks of society. This task begins in the nursery and goes on through to the university. Whatever institution, large or small, famous or obscure, dedicates itself to the necessary and heavy job of teaching men to think deserves the gratitude of the whole human race.

But thinking is not enough. Men are made to *worship* also, to bow down and adore in the presence of the mystery inexpressible. Man's mind is not the top peak of his nature. Higher than his mind is his spirit, that something within him which can engage the supernatural, which under the breath of the Spirit can come alive and enter into conscious communion with heaven, can receive the divine nature and hear and feel and see the ineffable wonder that is God.

When, therefore, an institution dedicated to the growth and development of the thinking person seeks at the same time to turn this thinker into a worshipper, our debt to that institution becomes all the greater. So many schools on every level are content to train the intellect, forgetting that they are dealing with but part of the man – an important part certainly, but a part only. The wise of the world who have not learned to worship are but demi-men, unformed and rudimentary. Their further development awaits the life-giving touch of Christ to wake them into spiritual birth and life eternal.

But the thinking, worshipping man is still short of perfection until he becomes also the *working* man. In a world like ours there is and always will be plenty of important work for the thoughtful, reverent man to do. Morally the world is like a bombed city. The streets are blocked, the buildings lie in ruins and the wounded and homeless wait for the healing services of men and women who can help them in their distress.

No man can be said to be truly educated who cannot relate his intellectual gifts to creative work. And no work, however sacrificial, will be permanent unless it is geared to eternity. Only what is done in a spirit of worship will last for ever.

When the man becomes a thinking man a great deal

17

Truth Is a Great Treasure

To know the truth is the greatest privilege any man can enjoy in this life, as truth itself is without doubt the richest treasure anyone can possess.

This follows from the nature of truth, and from the world-outlasting dowry it brings to those who open their hearts to it.

Apart from truth our human lives would lose all their value, and we ourselves become no better than the beasts that perish.

Our response to truth should be eager and instant. We dare not dally with it; we dare not treat it as something we can obey or not obey, at our pleasure. It is a glorious friend, but it is nevertheless a hard master, exacting unquestioning obedience.

While a life lived in conformity with the truth will come at last to a good and peaceful end, candour requires us to admit that the lover of truth will have to endure many a heartache, many a sorrow as he journeys through the wilderness. This is the price the world makes him pay for the priceless privilege of obeying the truth. The world being what it is, truth must carry its own forfeit.

The servant of truth will be penalised for his devotion. So goes the world alway.

Any man who would escape the heavy tax which humankind lays upon the righteous must make a satisfactory compromise with error. This is so because sin has perverted the nature of things. 'He that departeth from evil maketh himself a prey' is as true now as when it was first uttered. Little as we like to admit it, two thousand years of Christianity have not made much difference. The human race is still cursed with what Bacon called 'a natural though corrupt love of the lie itself'.

Nevertheless the hazards of truth should not count in our final tally. Truth is such a royal patron that we should embrace it without regard to cost. The cautious calculator, who tinkers with truth for fear of consequences, is no worthy servant of such a noble master.

We Christians above all people should value truth, for we profess to belong to the one who is the Truth. The Stoics who had no access to the Scriptures nevertheless had a noble concept of truth and of man's responsiblity to it. When on trial for his life before a hostile and prejudiced court one of them told his accusers: 'A man who is good for anything ought not to calculate the chance of living or dying; he ought only to consider whether in doing anything he is doing right or wrong – acting the part of a good man or a bad.'

The true follower of Christ will not ask, 'If I embrace this truth, what will it cost me?' Rather he will say, 'This is truth, God help me to walk in it, let come what may!'

18

The Blessedness of the Fixed Heart

It will probably be found at last that there is no sin except sin of the mind.

It is the carnal mind that is enmity against God, that is not subject to the law of God, neither can be. It should, however, be remembered that when the Bible speaks of the mind it does not refer to the intellect alone. The whole personality is included in the concept; the bent of the will, the moral responses, the sympathies and antipathies are there also, as well as the intellect.

When God saw the wickedness of man, that it was great in the earth, He saw what could not be seen from the outside, that, as it is rendered in one place, 'the whole imagination, with the purposes and desires of the heart' was only evil continually (see Genesis 6:5). From this passage alone we may properly gather that sin has its seat deep within the mind where it pollutes the emotions (desires), the intellect (imaginations) and the will (purposes). These taken together constitute what the Bible and popular theology call the heart.

It is significant that when our Lord describes the stream of iniquity as it flows out of the heart He begins with the thoughts. 'For out of the heart proceed evil thoughts, murders, adulteries, fornications, thefts, false witness, blasphemies' (Matthew 15:19). It is doubtful whether any sin is ever committed until it first incubates in the thoughts long enough to stir the feelings and predispose the will toward it favourably. Even the sudden flash of anger, which of all sins would appear on the surface to have the lowest mental content is anything but a sudden eruption of the emotions. The 'quick-tempered' man is one who habitually broods over wrongs and insults and thus conditions himself for the sudden fit of temper that seems to have no mental origin. The heart that has had the benefit of broad, sane thinking on moral questions, especially long meditation upon man's sin, God's mercy and the goodness of Christ in dying for His enemies, is not conditioned to blow up when occasion arises. The worst reaction to an affront or an injustice will be annoyance or mild irritation, never a burst of sinful anger.

The Old Testament tells how the wicked man lies in his bed thinking out ways to do evil and when the morning comes carries out the plans he has made during the night 'because it is in the power of (his) hand.' And the psalmist exhorts us, 'Stand in awe, and sin not: commune with your own heart upon your bed, and be still' (Psalm 4:4). What can this mean but that moral conduct, good or bad, originates deep within the mind? The thoughts dwell upon an act or course of action with interest and consent; this stirs the affections which in turn trigger off the will to the act under contemplation. The sin that follows may be so base, so physical, so obviously 'of the flesh' that no one would dream it began as an undisciplined thought in the heart. The rich fool 'thought within himself' and as a result took a course that cost him his soul (Luke 12:16–21).

All our acts are born out of our minds and will be what the mind is at last. This is clearly taught in the Word:

'Keep thy heart with all diligence; for out of it are the issues of life.' Even repentance must begin with deep reverent thought. David said, 'I thought on my ways, and turned my feet unto thy testimonies' (Psalm 119:59), and it is plain that the prodigal son thought things over very seriously before he could get the consent of his will to humble himself and say, 'I will arise and go to my father, and will say unto him, Father, I have sinned' (Luke 15:11–32).

It is something of a happy paradox that while the thoughts deeply affect the will and go far to determine its choices, the will on the other hand has the power to control the thoughts. A will firmly engaged with God can swing the intellectual powers around to think on holy things. Were it not so, Paul's words to the Philippians would be psychologically untenable: 'Finally, brethren, whatsoever things are true, whatsoever things are honest, whatsoever things are just, whatsoever things are pure, whatsoever things are lovely, whatsoever things are of good report; if there be any virtue, and if there be any praise, think on these things' (Philippians 4:8). Since we are here commanded to think on certain things it follows that we can command our thoughts; and if we can pick the objects upon which to meditate we can in the end sway our whole inner life in the direction of righteousness.

It is much more important that we think godly thoughts and will to do God's will than that we feel 'spiritual'. Religious feelings may and do vary so greatly from person to person, or even in the same person they may vary so widely from one time to the next, that it is never safe to trust them. Let us by a determined act of faith set our affections on things above and God will see to the rest. The safest, and after a while the happiest, man is the one who can say, 'My heart is fixed, trusting in the Lord.'

19

How the Lord Leads

One of the problems most frequently encountered by serious-minded Christians is how to discover the will of God in a given situation.

This is not a small matter. To countless thousands of Christians it is vitally important. Their peace of heart depends upon knowing that God is actually guiding them, and their failure to be sure that He is destroys their inward tranquillity and fills them with uncertainty and fear. They must get help if they are to regain their confidence. Here is a modest effort to provide some help.

First, it is absolutely essential that we be completely dedicated to God's high honour and surrendered to the lordship of Jesus Christ. God will not lead us except for His own glory and He cannot lead us if we resist His will. The shepherd cannot lead a stubborn sheep. The evil practice of *using* God must be abandoned. Instead of trying to employ God to achieve our ends we must submit ourselves joyously to God and let Him work through us to achieve His own ends.

Now, granted that we are wholly committed to God with every full intent to obey Him, we may expect actually to be led by Him. The Scriptures that teach us this are so many that one scarcely knows where to begin quoting. It only remains for us to believe they mean what they say.

The many choices that we Christians must make from day to day involve only four kinds of things: Those concerning which God has said an emphatic *no*; those about which He has said an equally emphatic *yes*; those concerning which He wants us to consult our own sanctified preferences; and those few and rare matters about which we cannot acquire enough information to permit us to make intelligent decisions and which for that reason require some special guidance from the Lord to prevent us from making serious mistakes.

Regardless of what our 'positive thinkers' have said, the Scriptures have much to say about things Christians are *not* to do. Every call to repentance is a call to negative as well as to positive moral action. 'Cease to do evil; learn to do well' (Isaiah 1:16, 17) is a fair epitome of the moral teaching of the Bible.

Put this down as an unfailing rule: Never seek the leading of the Lord concerning an act that is forbidden in the Word of God. To do so is to convict ourselves of insincerity.

Again, prophet, psalmist, apostle and our blessed Lord Himself join to point out the way of positive obedience. His yoke is easy, His burden is light and He giveth more grace, so let this be the second rule: Never seek the leading of the Lord concerning an act that has been commanded in the Scriptures.

Now, a happy truth too often overlooked in our anxious search for the will of God is that in the majority of decisions touching our earthly lives God expresses no choice, but leaves everything to our own preference. Some Christians walk under a cloud of uncertainty, worrying about which profession they should enter, which car they should drive, which school they should attend, where they should live and a dozen or score of other such matters, when their Lord has set them free to follow their own personal bent, guided only by their love for Him and for their fellow men.

On the surface it appears more spiritual to seek God's leading than just to go ahead and do the obvious thing. But it is not. If God gave you a watch would you honour Him more by asking Him for the time of day or by consulting the watch? If God gave a sailor a compass would the sailor please God more by kneeling in a frenzy of prayer to persuade God to show him which way to go or by steering according to the compass?

Except for those things that are specifically commanded or forbidden, it is God's will that we be free to exercise our own intelligent choice. The shepherd will lead the sheep but he does not wish to decide which tuft of grass the sheep shall nibble each moment of the day. In almost everything touching our common life on earth God is pleased when we are pleased. He wills that we be as free as birds to soar and sing our Maker's praise without anxiety. God's choice for us may not be *one* but *any one* of a score of possible choices. The man or woman who is wholly and joyously surrendered to Christ cannot make a wrong choice. Any choice will be the right one.

But what about those rare times when a great deal is at stake, we can discover no clear scriptural instruction and yet are forced to choose between two possible courses? In such a situation we have God's faithful promise to guide us aright. Here, for instance, are two passages from the Word of the Lord: 'If any of you lack wisdom, let him ask of God, that giveth to all men liberally, and upbraideth not; and it shall be given him. But let him ask in faith, nothing wavering' (James 1:5, 6). 'Thus saith the Lord, thy Redeemer, the Holy One of Israel; I am the Lord thy God which teacheth thee to profit, which leadeth thee by the way that thou shouldest go' (Isaiah 48:17).

Take your problem to the Lord. Remind Him of these promises. Then get up and do what looks best to you. Either choice will be right. God will not permit you to make a mistake.

20

Our Business Is God

If we could bring together in one huge directory a list of all the organisations, great and small, that exist throughout the earth for the promotion of special interests we would be astounded at the number of them.

Almost everything that human beings do or can do has its organisation, association, society or guild to focus attention upon it and promote its ends. Some of these are good, some are bad, most of them are just neutral; but each one, however boring or comical it may appear to those who are not interested, has its starry-eyed devotees who live for it alone and who derive their keenest pleasure from their preoccupation with it.

In the midst of all this there is one group of persons whose absorbing interest is, or should be, God. That group is the Church.

The Church is born out of the gospel and that gospel has to do with God and man's relation to God. Christianity engages to bring God into human life, to make men right with God, to give them a heart knowledge of God, to teach them to love and obey God and ultimately to restore in them the lost image of God in full and everlasting perfection.

Our Lord, in defining eternal life, summed up the supreme goal of human existence: That they might know thee the only true God, and Jesus Christ, whom thou hast sent.' And Paul revealed the one overpowering interest of his life when he wrote, 'That I may know him.'

The business of the Church is God. She is purest when most engaged with God and she is astray just so far as she follows other interests, no matter how 'religious' or humanitarian they may be.

There are a thousand useful, even noble, pursuits in which the Church may engage and which may bring her the plaudits of the world but which are nevertheless unworthy of her utter devotion. Such are social activities for their own sake, philosophical pursuits divorced from Him in whom all wisdom and knowledge is hidden away, art, music, education, travel, to name a mere few. As these things come to the Christian in his pursuit of God they may have a proper and useful place in his life; but when they are chosen as ends to be followed they are and can only be cheap substitutes for the glory that excelleth.

For choosing God as our one all-absorbing interest we Christians are sometimes scorned or written off as hopelessly narrow-minded. But must we apologise? Must we apologise that we have chosen Christ as our career? That we deliberately will to walk with those who walk with God? That we have chosen eternity over time and heaven over earth? Must we apologise that we have chosen to seek good and not evil all the days of our lives? That we have chosen so to live that we dare to die?

In so choosing whom have we injured? Whose son or daughter is the worse for knowing us? Whose house have we robbed or whose money have we stolen? Whom have we led into crime? Who is a worse husband or father or citizen for following our Saviour? If we have wronged anyone it is in spite of our Christian faith, not

because of it. No man, no home, no nation is the worse
for the presence of a real Christian.

Gerhard Tersteegen, the saintly silk weaver, said it for
us in a delightful little bit of verse:

Child of the Eternal Father,
   Bride of the Eternal Son,
Dwelling place of God the Spirit,
   Thus with Christ made ever one;
Dowered with joy beyond the angels,
   Nearest to His throne,
They the ministers attending His beloved one:
   Granted all my heart's desire,
All things made my own;
   Feared by all the powers of evil,
Fearing God alone;
   Walking with the Lord in glory
Through the courts divine,
   Queen within the royal palace,
Christ for ever mine:
Say, poor worldling, can it be
That my heart should envy thee?

21

We Must Depend upon the Holy Spirit

Because we are the kind of persons we are and because we live in a world such as we do, the shepherd of souls is often forced to work at what would appear to be cross purposes with himself.

For instance, he must encourage the timid and warn the self-confident; and these may at any given time be present in his congregation in almost equal numbers. His effort to encourage those who need encouragement may actually confirm presumptuous souls in their carelessness. Conversely, his much needed warnings and reproofs may drive timorous and doubting Christians to the borders of despair.

Another problem he faces is the presence, in the normal Christian assembly, of believers in every stage of development, from the newly converted who knows almost nothing about the Christian life to the wise and experienced Christian who seems to know almost everything.

Again, the Christian minister must have a word from God for the teen-aged, the middle-aged and the very aged. He must speak to the scholar as well as to the ignorant; he must bring the living Word to the cultured man and woman and to the vulgarian who reads nothing but the sports page and the comic strip. He must speak to the sad and to the happy, to the tender-minded and to the tough-minded, to those eager to live and to some who secretly wish they could die. And he must do this all in one sermon and in a period of time not exceeding 45 minutes. Surely this requires a Daniel, and Daniels are as scarce today as in Babylon in 600 BC.

To add to the pastor's burden is the knowledge that in each service there will likely be a few lost sons who should come home, some who never loved God at all and 'some who lost the love they had'. So he must call sinners to repentance, warn the unruly, comfort the feeble-minded, instruct, reprove, rebuke, encourage, console and exhort all at the same time, or at least on the same day.

This is the situation stated baldly, but it is not actually as difficult as it looks. I said that the preacher *appears* to be at cross purposes with himself; but it is in appearance only, for what seems to be confusion is but the seamy side of the tapestry. The artistic pattern is on the other side.

The man of God may labour on in complete trust and in full expectation of success, provided he is aware of a few basic truths. One is that however different people may be in externals, they are all alike fundamentally. That in us to which the Christian message is directed is the same in every human being.

Before the cross of Jesus we are not old or young, educated or ignorant, cultured or uncouth, dull or brilliant; we are just people – human beings lost and ruined deep inside where incidental differences do not matter, where indeed they are not even known. As gold is gold whether it is mixed with the sand of the stream or wrought into an exquisite work of art by the hand of a Cellini, so the essential stuff of human nature is the same under whatever conditions it may be found. That about us which yields itself to social differentiation, is not that for which Christ died. He did not, for example, die for doctors, farmers, authors, labourers, artists, engineers, professors, vagrants, presidents, musicians, lumbermen; He died for *lost humanity*, and any one can receive the benefits of His atonement, *but only as lost beings*. Colour, race, social standings, occupation, cultural levels do not count, for they do not alter the basic human thing for which His blood was shed.

Because the inner lostness is the same in all human beings, the work of God to reclaim them must be the same in all. And the Spirit broods over all, illuminating, revealing, convicting, enabling them to hear and see and understand.

It is one of the wonders and delights of preaching that the same message will often affect people differently, producing in one repentance, in another hope, in still others courage, humility or faith, according as the particular soul has need.

Without this mighty, skillful working of the Spirit, preaching would be futile; with it the ministry of the Word can be easy and delightful as well as marvellously effective.

22

Beware the Prophets
of Tranquillity

Over the years I have read or thumbed through a great many books on how to conquer fear. The cult of relaxation has, in fact, quite taken over certain areas of the religious thinking of the day.

Of course the fear-not cultists are able to assemble a lot of Scripture to support their teaching, but the catch is that practically all of it is misunderstood or misapplied. It just doesn't mean what they say it does, and what is still worse, it isn't addressed to the people they try to apply it to.

The fear-not philosophers all begin with the same error; namely, that there is nothing to fear, and all we need to do to get deliverance is to believe it. To teach people living in a world like ours that there is nothing to be afraid of is to be guilty of gross irresponsibility and any teacher who does so disqualifies himself instantly and proves himself unworthy of the confidence of serious-minded men.

Both the Bible and human experience teach that the world is full of enemies to mankind, not the least of those dangers being man himself. Our Lord said, 'I will forewarn you whom you shall fear: Fear him, which after he hath killed hath power to cast into hell; yea, I say unto you, Fear him.'

A sinful man *should* be afraid; he has plenty to be afraid of. The consequences of his sins, death, judgement and hell are all awaiting him and he cannot escape them by looking the other way. While he lives on earth there are dangers of every kind facing him and everyone he loves. Any religious teacher that exhorts him to ignore these dangers is unrealistic, false to the facts and a deadly enemy to his soul. The prophet of tranquillity is indeed another source of danger to him and should be considered one more object of fear.

Where there are mortal perils and no place to hide, fear is the only sane reaction. To dismiss fear while the danger still exists is little short of insanity. Until the danger has been removed, fear should remain. Only that man has a right to be unafraid who has fled for refuge to the mighty Saviour. Such a man knows the danger is there, but also knows that his Almighty Lord will bring him safely through and present him at last faultless before the presence of God.

There are in the Scriptures innumerable exhortations to put away fear; but they are all addressed to God's own children, never to the children of this world. Someone must care, and if a man has not cast his fears on Christ, he must bear them himself. The safety of the rock is for those who have put their trust in the rock. All others must face their enemies alone.

23

Christ Is All We Need

One thing the young Christian should be taught as quickly as possible after his conversion is that Jesus Christ is all he needs. When he believes effectively on Christ as his Lord and Saviour he can humbly declare his independence of everyone and everything outside of Christ.

This the New Testament teaches with great emphasis and clarity and with fullness of detail. We need not quote any proof text in support of this statement, but suggest simply that the inquirer read the Scriptures to see for himself, especially John, Ephesians, Colossians and Hebrews.

One marked characteristic of modern evangelicalism is its lack of assurance, resulting in a pathetic search for external evidence to corroborate its faith. It sets out bravely to declare its trust in Christ, but is shortly overawed by the counter declarations of science and philosophy and before long it is looking hesitantly about for some collateral evidence to restore its confidence.

Our frantic and futile effort to harmonise the truth of Christ with psychology, philosophy and science is proof enough of a deep incertitude among us concerning the sufficiency of Christ. It is a tragicomic sight to see our modern apostles licking the palm of any man of learning who will condescend to say something complimentary about Jesus Christ. How eagerly we rush into print with any quotation from the lips of the Great Man of the world that can be tortured into an admission that he believes that Jesus is the Son of God.

The New Testament points to Christ and says God now commands all men everywhere to repent: because He has appointed a day, in which He will judge the world in righteousness by that man whom He has ordained; whereof He has given assurance unto all men, in that He has raised Him from the dead. God validated for ever the claims of Christ. He is *who* He said He was and *what* He said He was. Christ stands before no man to be judged, but every man stands before Him. Any uncertainty about Him was swept away for ever when He arose from the dead, ascended into heaven and sent down the Holy Spirit as His final witness among men. Now it may be said that Christ as the second person of the Godhead is self-validating. He needs no supplementary witness from the world of nature or from the race of men. He is His own witness.

The faith of the Christian rests upon Christ Himself. On Him we repose and in Him we live. Christ gains nothing from any human philosophy, however pure and noble it may be. He owes nothing to Plato or to Aristotle. If these men had never lived the Christ in whom dwells all the fullness of the Godhead bodily would have been all He ever was and is world without end. His redemptive work was completed centuries before the dawn of modern science, and of course seeks no aid from science. Christ is unique in the only sense that word will bear. He is the mystery of Godliness, a miracle, an emergence of the Deity into time and space for a reason and a purpose. He is complete in Himself.

Because we Christians live on two life-levels simultaneously, the spiritual and the natural, we do, as sons of Adam, owe to philosophy and science a lasting debt of gratitude. Music, literature, art, statecraft, economics, learning contribute to our welfare and make the world a more comfortable place in which to live while we wait for the manifestation of the sons of God and the redemption of our bodies. So it is good that we gain all the knowledge we can in the short time that is ours. Whatever we learn that is true will remain our treasured possession in the world to come. For these reasons I believe in education, as full as possible for as many as possible as quickly as possible.

That is one thing. It is quite another to try to equate the faith of Christ with philosophy or science or any other or all of the products of superior human minds. And to make that faith dependent upon these things is in the light of Christ's deity not only preposterous but near to sacrilegious. Christ is enough. To have Him and nothing else is to be rich beyond conceiving. To have all else and have not Christ is to be a cosmic pauper, cut off for ever from all that will matter at last.

The apostle said it well: 'But of him are ye in Christ Jesus, who of God is made unto us wisdom, and righteousness, and sanctification, and redemption: that, according as it is written, He that glorieth let him glory in the Lord' (1 Corinthians 1:30–31).

24

We Need to Elevate Our Sights

There are few things as frustrating as to work without knowing what we are trying to accomplish; that is, to be lost in the means and ignorant of the end.

Examples of this are found in 'parts' factories where men spend years making small articles that have no significance in themselves and can have satisfying meaning only when related to hundreds of other and dissimilar articles and to the completed object of which each one is a small part.

Since the human mind is designed to deal with ends and wholes, this enforced preoccupation with parts and means is particularly disconcerting. The urge to plan and to create according to plan is strong in us, and we feel fenced in and defeated when we are compelled to spend our days in toil that attains no visible objective. It is this rather than the work itself that makes so many jobs dull and boring.

I have wondered whether the flat tedium found in most churches cannot be explained at least in part as the psychological consequence of numbers of persons meeting together at stated times without quite knowing why they have met. Most people simply do not like to go to church and will not go if they can escape the ordeal decently; and millions can and do.

It would be too easy to dismiss this dislike for church as only another symptom of original sin and love of moral darkness, but I believe that explanation is too pat to be wholly true. It doesn't explain enough. Some persons, for instance, find church intolerable because there is no objective toward which pastor and people are moving, aside possibly from the limited one of trying to enlist eight more women and ten more men to chaperon the annual youth barbecue or reaching the building fund quota for the month. And believe me, that can get mighty wearisome after a while, so wearisome indeed that alert, forward-looking persons often forsake the churches in droves and leave the spiritless, the dull and those afflicted with permanent insouciance to carry on, if a phrase so active dare be used to describe what they do.

To Paul there was nothing dull or tiresome in the religion of Christ. God had a plan which was being carried forward to completion, and Paul and 'all the faithful in Christ Jesus' were part of that plan. It included predestination, redemption, adoption and the obtaining of an eternal inheritance in the heavenly places. God's purpose has now been openly revealed (Ephesians 3:10, 11).

It was the knowledge that they were part of an eternal plan that imparted unquenchable enthusiasm to the early Christians. They burned with holy zeal for Christ and felt that they were part of an army which the Lord was leading to ultimate conquest over all the powers of darkness. That was enough to fill them with perpetual enthusiasm.

It is one of the anomalies of religion in our day that the orthodox churches appear to have lost their crusading spirit (obviously for want of a crusade), and the enthusiasm they once had and lost has gone over to a false religion and an evil political system. I refer of course to Russellism and Communism.

Communism is an evil, but it drives on toward world domination for the very reason that its devotees are convinced that it is destined to dominate. It is this conviction that makes Communists all but invincible. Any act one of them may perform for the cause carries an emotional warhead: it is the fixed belief that his act is part of a high plan that more than justifies it.

Russellism (now travelling under the alias of Jehovah's Witnesses) is also motivated by a clear purpose. Its followers talk with starry-eyed fervour about the 'kingdom' and, however far they may have strayed from the truth, they are nevertheless *convinced* that they are sons of a new world order soon to emerge. To them this new order is completely real and in their enthusiasm they care little how many persons they offend or how many enemies they make. In the light of their glorious future nothing else matters. So they believe and their belief, though false, furnishes all the drive they need.

The evangelical Christian need make no apology for his beliefs. They are in direct lineal descent from those of the apostles. He can check the tenets of his total creed against the life-giving, transforming beliefs of church fathers both East and West, reformers, mystics, missionaries, saints and evangelists, and they will check out one by one. Then let him check them all with the Holy Scriptures and again they will prove to be sound.

What then is the trouble? Why the inertia, the torpor that lies over the church?

The answer is that we are too comfortable, too rich, too contented. We hold the faith of our fathers, but it does not hold us. We are suffering from judicial blindness visited upon us because of our sins. To us has been committed the most precious of all treasures, but we are not committed to it. We insist upon making our religion a form of amusement and will have fun whether or not. We are afflicted with religious myopia and see only things near at hand.

God has set eternity in our hearts and we have chosen time instead. He is trying to interest us in a glorious tomorrow and we are settling for an inglorious today. We are bogged down in local interests and have lost sight of eternal purposes. We improvise and muddle along, hoping for heaven at last but showing no eagerness to get there, correct in doctrine but weary of prayer and bored with God.

the outgoing students and by their smiling and misty-eyed parents can be understood only when we remember that people like to hear what they want to hear and at a time like that they are not willing to spoil the pleasure of it by checking on the accuracy of anything they are told.

The fact is that men have never in any numbers sought after truth. If we may judge people's interests by their deeds, then of the young men and women who stream forth from our halls of learning each year the vast majority have no more than a passing and academic interest in truth. They go to college not to satisfy a yearning to discover truth, but to improve their social standing and increase their earning power. These motives are not necessarily to be despised; but they should be known for what they are, and not hidden beneath a pink cloud of specious idealism.

What are people actually seeking? Of course they seek satisfaction for the basic urges such as hunger, sex and social companionship; but beyond these what? Certainly for nothing as high and noble as truth.

Ask the average person what he wants from life and if he is candid he will tell you he wants success in his chosen field; and he wants success both for the prestige it brings him and for the financial security it affords. And why does he want financial security? To guarantee him against the loss of comforts, luxuries and pleasures, which he believes are rightfully his as a part of his heritage. The ominous thing about all this is that *everything he wants can be bought with money*. It would be hard to think of an indictment more terrible than that.

The notion that the world is full of truth seekers becomes stronger as we approach the church and mingle with religious persons. The liberal and humanistic churches bear down especially hard on this point, their ministers constantly flattering their listeners that they are engaged in a heroic quest for the truth. That a few hundred persons will gather in a church building once a week to sit on cushioned pews and listen to good music appears to be enough to satisfy the too easily satisfied minister that his congregation is composed of crusaders of the first water.

Either to avoid embarrassment or because he is not sure of his own beliefs the said liberal minister is usually careful to avoid definitions, so no one knows exactly what it is he is supposed to be looking for. But it gives a tremendous lift to a man's self-respect to think of himself, if only briefly and once a week, as a lofty idealist searching for truth, a kind of cosmic prospector digging for gold among the hills of God. If his wife fails to recognise him by that description it really doesn't matter, for no one takes the whole thing very seriously anyway. But it is a relief from the grind of business, traffic and taxes.

The world is full of seekers, true enough, and they gravitate quite naturally toward the church. Seekers after peace of mind are plentiful enough to keep the printing presses busy; seekers after physical health are always with us in sufficient numbers to make our leading faith healers comfortably rich; seekers after success and safety are legion, as our popular religious leaders know too well. But real seekers after truth are almost as rare as albino deer. And here is why:

Truth is a glorious but hard master. It makes moral demands upon us. It claims the sovereign right to control us, to strip us, even to slay us as it chooses. Truth will never stoop to be a servant but requires that all men serve it. It never flatters men and never compromises with them. It demands all or nothing and refuses to be used or patronised. It will be all in all or it will withdraw into silence.

It was Christ who capitalised truth and revealed that it

26

The Sovereignty of Truth – 2

It is born in every man to want to dramatise his life and to cast himself as the star of the performance.

Once let a man become persuaded that he is a hero in quest of the holy grail of truth and he becomes a victim of a pretty and pleasant delusion that inflates his ego and blinds him to the very truth he claims to seek. And if he is later forced to admit that he has not found it he absolves himself from all guilt, for has he not searched? Has he not hunted through the years for the precious treasure? Where is the stone he has left unturned? Where has he not drilled or dug among the philosophies and religions of the world? Why then has he not found?

To him there can be only one answer: The Spirit and Wisdom of the universe has let him down. The great Oversoul has withheld the secret from him. So he tells himself and in wounded dignity walks stiffly into the sunset convinced that he has been deeply wronged in his effort to discover life's *summum bonum*. His is a tragedy worthy of Aeschylus and he himself grand in failure and noble in defeat.

Disillusioning people is a thankless task and quite plainly does not come under the category of making friends and thinking positively. Nevertheless it must be done if we are to rescue lost men from the consequences of their delusions. So let me say boldly that it is not the difficulty of discovering truth but the unwillingness to obey it that makes it so rare among men.

Our Lord said, 'I am the truth,' and again He said, 'The Son of man is come to seek and to save that which was lost.' Truth therefore is not hard to find for the very reason that it is seeking us. Truth is not a thing for which we must search, but a person to whom we must hearken.

This is taught or taken for granted in the record of God's dealings with men throughout the sacred Scriptures. After the sin in Eden it was not Adam who cried 'O God, where art Thou?' but God who cried 'Where art thou?' as He sought for Adam among the trees of the Garden. Abraham heard God speak and responded, but it was God who was the aggressor. God appeared unto Jacob before Jacob came to appear before God. And in the burning bush God revealed Himself to Moses.

Again and again did God take the initiative. He sought for Gideon and found him on the threshing floor of Ophrah. He showed Himself to Isaiah when there is no evidence that Isaiah was seeking Him. Before Jeremiah was born God laid His hand upon him, and He opened heaven to let the discouraged priest Ezekiel see a vision and hear a voice. Amos said he was not a prophet neither a prophet's son, but the Lord 'took' him as he followed the flock. Again God was the aggressor.

In the New Testament things are not otherwise. True, multitudes came to Christ for physical help, but only rarely did one seek Him out to learn the truth; and even that rare one usually turned away when the truth was told him. The whole picture in the Gospels is one of a seeking Saviour, not one of seeking men. The truth was hunting for those who would receive it, and relatively few did. 'Many are called, but few are chosen.'

The truth, in the person of the Logos, the Word, is seeking to illuminate the minds of men. 'That was the true Light, which lighteth every man that cometh into the world.' For this reason, when we conceive ourselves to be honest seekers who cannot find the light we are in a state of dangerous self-deception. It is a grave situation. Unless help comes quickly the darkness may close down upon us permanently. 'If therefore the light that is in thee be darkness, how great is that darkness.'

Behind all our failure to find light is an unconfessed and possibly an unconscious love of darkness. 'This is the condemnation, that light is come into the world, and men loved darkness rather than light, because their deeds were evil. For every one that doeth evil hateth the light, neither cometh to the light, lest his deeds should be reproved. But he that doeth truth cometh to the light, that his deeds may be made manifest, that they are wrought in God' (John 3:19–21).

We should always remember that we are accountable not only for the light we have but also for the light we might have if we were willing to obey it. Truth is sovereign and will not allow itself to be trifled with. And it is easy to find for it is trying to find us. Obedience is the big problem: and unwillingness to obey is the cause of continued darkness.

27

What About the Ethics of Jesus?

A generation or so ago when Modernism was rising in religious circles, a great deal was heard about the ethics of Jesus and the tragic failure of the Church to get those ethics accepted by society.

The assumption was that our Lord had introduced into the world a superior system of ethics, based upon love and leading to brotherhood, and that His plan was to spread this new doctrine through the agency of the Church till throughout the whole wide world men 'should brothers be, for a' that and a' that'.

It may seem a bit odd that the religious teachers who exalted the teachings of Jesus to the seventh empyrean should in the same breath demote the person of Jesus to the level of a common man; yet they did just that. They lamented with many a crocodile tear the error of the Church in worshipping Jesus and failing to spread His ethics throughout the earth. The implication was that the man Jesus was important only because of the sterling quality of His ethics; though it was hard for some then and it is hard for others now to understand how a man's teaching can be greater than the man. The same persons who exalted His doctrine of love completely ignored His claim to deity and brushed aside His teachings on sin, judgement and hell, as well as His whole system of eschatology. This arrogant picking and choosing among the words of Christ gave some persons the impression that these teachers were far less sincere than they claimed to be, for a man need not be a genius to reach the conclusion that if Jesus was wrong about almost all of His teachings there could be no certainty that He was right about the rest.

Well, it is not my intention to fight again the battle of Bunker Hill. If all this belonged only to the past we might be content to let the dead bury their dead and pass on to something else; but the ghosts of the old Modernists appear to have been reincarnated and many of the arguments raised by the liberals a generation ago are now being repeated by the orthodox.

The ethics of Jesus must be imposed upon society, we are told, then all inequalities will vanish; the division of humanity into rich and poor, great and small, privileged and underprivileged will be no more. Under the benign influence of Christ's ethics of love, greed and war will disappear from the earth and the dream of universal brotherhood be realised at last.

Behind such teachings lie several grave errors, possibly the worst being the failure to distinguish the Church of Christ from the fallen world of mankind. According to the Bible the human race is morally fallen, spiritually alienated from God, lost and under the severe sentence of divine judgement. In sharp contrast to this, the Church is a body of regenerated persons who have withdrawn from the world in spirit and in heart and have thrown in their lot with Christ to own Him as Saviour and to follow Him as Lord.

Between these two groups, the world and the Church, there is a gulf as wide as space. The truly regenerated man is a new creature; he belongs to another order of being; he has another kind of life, another origin, another destiny. He is like those who sailed in the ark of Noah touching the watery world of lost men, to be sure, but separated from it by a thin hull that might as well have been miles thick, for it kept them in and kept the judgement water out.

The teachings of Jesus belong to the Church, not to society. In society is sin and sin is hostility to God. Christ did not teach that He would impose His teachings upon the fallen world. He called *His disciples* to Him and taught them, and everywhere throughout His teachings there is the overt or implied idea that His followers will constitute an unpopular minority group in an actively hostile world.

The divine procedure is to go into the world of fallen men, preach to them the necessity to repent and become disciples of Christ and, after making disciples, to teach them the 'ethics of Jesus', which Christ called 'all things whatsoever I have commanded you'.

The ethics of Jesus cannot be obeyed or even understood until the life of God has come to the heart of a man in the miracle of the new birth. The righteousness of the law is fulfilled in them who walk in the Spirit. Christ lives again in His redeemed follower the life He lived in Judaea; for righteousness can never be divorced from its source, which is Jesus Christ Himself.

The dream of a universal brotherhood based upon the ethics of Jesus is just that – a dream. It is compounded of a few words of Christ mixed with vast numbers of un-inspired words spoken by men whose yearnings are to be commended but whose wisdom is suspect. To arrive at the doctrine of brotherhood it is necessary that we reject the major portion of the New Testament and misunder-stand the rest.

There were once two brothers. They lived in a society that had not had time to develop the many social evils we know today. Yet one killed the other because sin was there. If two brothers in the morning of the world could not get on together, how can we hope that the gentle teachings of Jesus can ever bring brotherhood to a race filled with complex iniquities, where men inherit hates and where the souls of all are lacerated by jealousy, envy, egotism, greed and lust?

The hope of the individual is the new birth and acceptance of the teachings of Christ as a way of life. The hope of the race is that Christ shall come again to earth. *Even so, Lord, come quickly*.

28

We Have Lost Our Way

Among the many wonders of the Holy Scriptures is their ability frequently to compress into a sentence truth so vast, so complex, as to require a whole shelf of books to expound.

Even a single phrase may glow with a light like that of the ancient pillar of fire and its shining may illuminate the intellectual landscape for miles around.

An example is found in Jeremiah 10:23. After the Lord has spoken of the vanity of idols and had set in contrast to the gods of the heathen the glory of the living God, the King of Eternity, the prophet responded in an inspired exclamation that very well states the whole problem of humankind: 'O Lord, I know that the way of man is not in himself: it is not in man that walketh to direct his steps.'

The prophet here turns to a figure of speech, one which appears in the Scriptures so frequently that it is not easy to remember that it is but a figure. Man is seen as a traveller making his difficult way from a past he can but imperfectly recollect into a future about which he knows nothing. And he cannot stay, but must each morning strike his moving tent and journey on toward –

and there is the heavy problem – toward what?

It is a simple axiom of the traveller that if he would arrive at the desired destination he must take the right road. How far a man may have travelled is not important; what matters is whether or not he is going the right way, whether the path he is following will bring him out at the right place at last. Sometimes there will be an end to the road, and maybe sooner than he knows; but when he has gone the last step of the way will he find himself in a tomorrow of light and peace, or will the day toward which he journeys be 'a day of trouble and distress, a day of wasteness and desolation, a day of darkness and gloominess, a day of clouds and thick darkness'?

The inspired prophet Jeremiah says (and for that matter all the holy prophets who have spoken since the world began say) and our Lord and His apostles say that man does not know the way; indeed he hardly knows where he should go, to say nothing of the way he should take to get there. The worried Thomas spoke for every man when he asked, 'Lord, we know not whither thou goest; and how can we know the way?'

That is the truth and we had better face it squarely: the way of man is not in himself. However severe the blow to our pride, we would do well to bow our heads and admit our ignorance. For those who know not and know they know not, there may in the mercy of God be hope: for those who think they know there can be only increasing darkness.

Philosophically man has lost his way. Could he think himself out of his age-old predicament he would long ago have done it, for the world has had more than enough serious-minded men of superior intellectual endowments to examine every rabbit path in all the meadows of human thought and to explore every forest and wilderness in search of the way.

Since the first fallen man got still long enough to think,

fallen men have been asking these questions, 'Whence came I? What am I? Why am I here? and Where am I going?' The noblest minds of the race have struggled with these questions to no avail. Did the answer lie somewhere hidden like a jewel it would surely have been uncovered, for the most penetrating minds of the race have searched for it. Not a foot of ground but has been spaded up, neither is there crevice or cave anywhere in the region of human experience but has been spied into thoroughly and often as the centuries passed. Yet the answers remain as securely hidden as if they did not exist.

Why is man lost philosophically? Because he is lost morally and spiritually. He cannot answer the questions life presents to his intellect because the light of God has gone out in his soul. The fearful indictment the Holy Ghost brings against mankind is summed up count by count in the opening chapters of Romans and the conduct of every man from earliest recorded history to the present moment is evidence enough to sustain the indictment.

'When they knew God, they glorified him not as God,' read the terrible words, 'neither were thankful; but became vain in their imaginations, and their foolish heart was darkened. Professing themselves to be wise, they became fools, and changed the glory of the un-corruptible God into an image made like to corruptible man, and to birds, and fourfooted beasts, and creeping things...who changed the truth of God into a lie.' On and on the devastating words flow, mounting in intensity till no one with any conscience left or any fear of moral consequences can stand to look the Judge in the face, but must cast down his guilty eyes and cry, 'Have mercy upon me, O God, according to thy loving-kindness: according to the multitude of thy tender mercies blot out my transgressions.'

Apart from the Scriptures we have no sure philosophy; apart from Jesus Christ we have no true knowledge of God; apart from the in-living Spirit we have no ability to live lives morally pleasing to God.

How wonderful that Christ could say, 'I am the way, the truth, and the life.' For this we can never be thankful enough.

29

Five Kinds of Seekers

The Greek philosopher Pythagoras is said to have divided men into three classes: 1. Seekers after knowledge. 2. Seekers after honour. 3. Seekers after gain.

This is obviously an arbitrary division made for convenience, and like all such divisions it is too general to be entirely accurate. Still it is the report of a widely travelled and brilliant observer, and for that reason if for no other it deserves from all of us respectful attention.

Pythagorus appeared in Greece near the beginning of that short but wonderfully fertile period which, before it spent itself, had given to the world such geniuses as Socrates, Plato, Aristotle and Zeno. While Pythagoras himself was a mathematician and astronomer he was also a man with strong religious bent, his religion taking the direction of high morality and leading him to found a religio-philosophic brotherhood dedicated to the reformation of the moral standards of society.

It would be interesting if not too edifying to look for Pythagoras's three classes in modern society.

1. *Seekers after knowledge.* These are no longer called philosophers, 'lovers of wisdom', but scholars, professors, scientists, who love knowledge for itself.

These are intellectual magpies with a compulsive tic that drives them to collect all the shiny bits of knowledge possible; fortunately for them there are enough others with the same tic to provide them with a means of making some kind of a living here below.

2. *Seekers after honour*. These are the politicians. They have an incurable itch to be known in the gates, and as a means toward this end they manage to work up a convincing if phony patriotic fever every election year that brings them votes and political power. Their reward is in being applauded by the masses they secretly despise, and verily they have their reward.

3. *Seekers after gain*. These are at the top honest businessmen who become wealthy within the law, and at the bottom racketeers who gain their wealth outside the law. Morally these latter differ not at all from the ordinary bandit, but they differ socially because they are smarter, have read a book and know a better lawyer.

Thus far Pythagoras. But I wonder why he failed to notice two other classes: those who are not seekers after anything and those who are seekers after God. These no doubt existed in Pythagoras's day as they do in ours and it is odd that he did not recognise them. Let us add them to the list.

4. *Seekers after nothing*. These are the human vegetables who live by their glands and their instincts. I refer not to those unfortunate persons who by birth or by accident have been deprived of their normal faculties. There but by the grace of God go I. I do refer to the millions of normal persons who have allowed their magnificent intellectual equipment to wither away from lack of exercise.

These seekers after nothing have certain large earmarks. They may be known by the company they keep. Their reading matter is the sports page and the comic section; their art is limited to magazine covers and the illustrated trivialities of the weekly picture magazines; their music is whatever is popular and handy and loud. After work they sit and watch television or just drive around waiting for – what?

It is an omen and a portent that this describes many of our population and that they constitute what we proudly call the 'electorate'; that is, they decide the direction our country shall go, morally, politically and religiously. *O tempora! O mores!*

5. *Seekers after God*. Thanks be to God on high that these too are among us. They are the salt of the earth and the light of the world. Their number is not large when counted against the millions who have forgotten their Maker, but taken together they are a goodly company and dear to the heart of God.

Ah, those God-hungry souls! By nature they are no better than the rest of men, and by practice they have sometimes been worse. The one sign of their divine election is their insatiable thirst after the source of their being. Deep calls unto deep and they hear and respond.

These are almost always a disappointment to themselves, and sometimes they have for a while been a stumbling block to the world, as were Jacob and David and Peter. But many waters cannot quench love, neither can the floods drown it, and their questing hearts find what they seek at last. The grace of God meets them as they return and changes them from what they are sorry they have been, into what they have so fervently longed to become.

Today we know what the wise Greek could not know, that God was in Christ reconciling the world unto Himself, not imputing their trespasses. Seekers after God there surely were even in those old Grecian times and their destiny lies in the hand of the One who gave His only-begotten Son to die for the life of the world.

One word needs to be added. It will go better in the

day of reckoning for the seeker of pre-Christian days who stretched out pagan hands toward God in hope that he might find Him, than for the careless sinner of today who is sated with hearing and who refuses to repent and believe.

30

Controversy May Have
Its Holy Uses

The devil is a master strategist. He varies his attacks as skillfully as an experienced general and always has one more trick to use against the one who imagines he is well experienced in holy war.

By two radically opposite things the devil seeks to destroy us – by our sins and by our virtues.

First, he tempts us to sin. This might be called his conventional device. It worked against Adam and Eve and still works after the passing of the centuries. By means of it millions each year are, as Paul said, drowned in destruction and perdition. One would think the human race would learn to resist the blandishments of its sworn enemy, and it probably would except that there is an enemy within the gate – the fallen heart is secretly on the side of the devil.

It is, however, Satan's wiliest strategem to use our virtues against us, and this he often does with astonishing success. By means of temptation to sin he strikes at our personal lives; by working through our virtues he gets at the whole community of believers and unfits it for its own defence.

A parallel to Satan's technique may be seen in the

activities of certain subversive political groups who use government constitutions as a shield while they work to destroy those same constitutions. By unctuous pleading for the right of free speech they seek to destroy all freedom of speech. By talking piously about government by law they push their country toward the place where there will be government by dictatorship and all laws will mean what a ruling clique of base, cynical men want them to mean. So diabolical is this method that one can only conclude that those who use it learned it from their father the devil, whose they are and whom they serve.

To capture a city an enemy must first weaken or destroy its resistance, and so it is with the evangelical forces at any given time or place. It is impossible for Satan to storm the citadel of God as long as faithful watchmen stand on the walls to rouse her soldiers to action. The Church will never fall as long as she resists. This the devil knows; consequently he uses any stratagem to neutralise her resistance.

Many times in history the Christians in various towns, cities and even whole countries have given up their defence for reasons wholly evil. Worldliness, sinful pleasures and personal ungodliness have often been the cause of the Church's disgraceful surrender to the enemy.

Today, however, Satan's strategy is different. Though he still uses the old methods where he can do so with success, his more effective method is to paralyse our resistance by appealing to our virtues, especially the virtue of charity.

He first creates a maudlin and wholly inaccurate concept of Christ as soft, smiling and tolerant. He reminds us that Christ was 'brought as a lamb to the slaughter, and as a sheep before her shearers is dumb, so he openeth not his mouth', and suggests that we go and do likewise. Then if we notice his foot in the door and rise to oppose him he appeals to our desire to be Christ-like. 'You must not practice negative thinking,' he tells us. 'Jesus said, "He that is not against me is for me." Also He said "Judge not," and how can you be a good Christian and pass adverse judgement on any religious talk or activity? Controversy divides the Body of Christ. Love is of God, little children, so love everybody and all will be well.'

Thus speaks the devil, using Holy Scripture falsely for his evil purpose; and it is nothing short of tragic how many of God's people are taken in by his sweet talk. The shepherd becomes afraid to use his club and the wolf gets the sheep. The watchman is charmed into believing that there is no danger, and the city falls to the enemy without a shot. So Satan destroys us by appealing to our virtues.

The clever proponents of evil political ideologies are spending millions to make us Americans ashamed to love our country. By the use of all available media of communication they are persuading our people that there is little left worth defending and certainly nothing worth dying for. They are building up in the public mind a picture of an American as a generous, tolerant, smiling chap who loves baseball and babies but is not too much concerned about 'fringe' political theories. This syn-thetic American subscribes to the doctrine of the father-hood of God and the brotherhood of man and let's go fishing – everything will be all right.

And so in religion, especially among the Protestants. Let a man rise to declare the unique lordship of Jesus Christ and the absolute necessity of obedience to Him and he is at once branded as a hatemonger and a divider of men. The devil has brainwashed large numbers of religious leaders so successfully that they are now too timid to resist him. And he, being the kind of devil he is, takes swift advantage of their cowardice to erect altars to Baal everywhere.

The Bible is a book of controversy. The Old Testament prophets were men of contention. Our Lord Jesus while on earth was in deadly conflict with the devil. The apostles, the Church fathers and the reformers were men of controversy. They fought the devil to the death and kept the torch of truth burning for all succeeding generations.

Is our contribution to history to be the ignoble one of letting the torch go out?

31

The True Motive for Christian Conduct

Selfish personal interest, says the Greek moral philosopher Epictetus, is the motive behind all human conduct.

By way of illustration he points to two dogs romping on the lawn with every appearance of friendship when suddenly someone tosses a piece of raw meat between them. Instantly their play turns into savage fight as each struggles to get the meat for himself. Their friendship lasts only as long as their interests coincide. When those interests conflict they become snarling enemies.

Let us not condemn the old thinker for comparing the conduct of men to that of animals. The Bible frequently does and, humbling as it may be to us, we humans often look bad by the comparison. 'Go to the ant, thou sluggard,' says the voice of God in the Proverbs, 'consider her ways, and be wise,' and the prophet Jeremiah says, 'Yea, the stork in the heaven knoweth her appointed times; and the turtle and the crane and the swallow observe the time of their coming; but my people know not the judgment of the Lord.'

The children of this world, Christ tells us, are often wiser than the children of light. In his discovery of the springs of human conduct Epictetus reveals an understanding of mankind far beyond that of the average Christian; and this in spite of the fact that the Christian claims to possess the Spirit of truth and the Greek did not.

If we would be wise in the wisdom of God we must face up to the truth no matter how uncomplimentary it may be to us. It would be more comfortable to shrug off what our eyes behold and loyally declare our belief in the intrinsic goodness of all men; but our eternal welfare forbids that we deal dishonestly with reality. The truth is, men are not basically good; they are basically evil, and the essence of their sin lies in their selfishness.

The putting of our own interests before the glory of God is sin in its Godward aspect, and the putting of our own interests before those of our fellow men is sin as it relates to society. We know men are sinners because when they must choose between others and themselves they choose themselves every time. Personal interest sees to that.

Whether we are considering two men or two nations we see how personal interest controls their relation to each other. Two men can live together in perfect harmony as long as their interests coincide. Indeed it might correctly be said that human society can exist only by organising itself in such a manner as to serve the interests of the majority of persons composing it, or at least of those persons who are in a position to fight for their rights.

As long as their interests do not conflict nations may for centuries live side by side in peace; when a shift in population or a change in the economic structure takes place nations that have been friends for generations may suddenly become enemies. Hostility between nations or blocks of nations can always be traced to a clash of personal interest. All wars arise out of a collision of interests and must for that reason be recognised as a manifestation of sin. 'From whence come wars and fight-ings among you?' asks James, 'come they not hence, even of your lusts that war in your members?'

Human society is built upon a balance of personal interests. People are so used to seeing everyone serving his own ends that no other kind of conduct is expected. Only the eccentric dreamer would expect that unregenerate men could be persuaded to surrender their personal rights and devote themselves wholly to the interests of others. Occasionally small groups of persons have come together to try to form a selfless society, but in every instance they have lived to see their little utopia tear itself apart by the centrifugal force generated by the very selfishness they were trying so nobly to escape. The human heart is essentially selfish and it canot be cured by external organisation.

With the advent of Jesus Christ a new and radically different motive for human conduct was introduced into the world and its symbol is the cross. By His words Christ exposed the evil of self-interest and by His cross He demonstrated pure selfless love in its fullest perfection. He came not to be ministered unto, but to minister, and to give His life a ransom for many. Christ pleased not Himself, but lived in total devotion to the honour of God and the welfare of mankind, and when He died He set a crown of beauty upon a God-centred and others-centred life.

The cross is a symbol of the selfless, others-centred life of Christ, but it does not end there. Our Lord made it also a symbol of the normal Christian life. 'If any man will come after me,' He said, 'let him deny himself, and take up his cross, and follow me. For whosoever will save his life shall lose it: and whosoever will lose his life for my sake shall find it.'

The teaching here is too plain to miss. The self-interest motive in our conduct, though it is inherent in fallen human nature, is nevertheless an evil and destructive thing that can lead at last only to tragic and everlasting loss. Love alone can make our conduct acceptable to God.

It is time we checked our brand of Christianity against the New Testament. There is real danger that we may overlook this radical new motive for human conduct and go on serving our own interests under a disguise of godliness. And that is a mistake none of us can afford to make.

32

Why Faith Is Indispensable

'Without faith it is impossible to please God' has become an axiom of the Christian way; yet I suppose not many stop to ask why faith should be so vitally important in our relation with God. But there is a reason.

This is a moral universe. At bottom it is not material, though it contains matter; it is not mathematical, though it involves numbers. The God who made the world is a moral being and He has filled His world with moral creatures.

We hear of mysterious beings who have access to the presence of God and who range throughout the whole creation as servants of the Most High. 'Bless the Lord, ye his angels, that excel in strength, that do his commandments, hearkening unto the voice of his word.' The Scriptures tell us of at least four orders of such beings and refer to what they call 'watchers and holy ones', which may indicate other orders or may simply refer to the previously mentioned four.

In addition, there is another and of course a more familiar order of being, the last and (before his fall) the highest of all the creatures God created and made. I refer to man who was made in God's image and likeness and who for that reason bears toward God a unique moral and spiritual relation.

Because this is a moral universe, character, which is the excellence of moral beings, is naturally paramount. As the excellence of steel is strength and the excellence of art is beauty, so the excellence of mankind is moral character. 'An honest man is the noblest work of God,' an apophthegm usually attributed to John Wesley, may sound at first rather extreme, but if we allow the word 'honest' to stand for all the moral virtues we may be able to understand the apophthegm and possibly to agree with it. A saint should be not only a man of intense spiritual devotion but a man of symmetrical virtues and perfectly balanced character.

Relationship between moral beings is by confidence and confidence rests upon character, which is a guarantee of conduct. It is true that sin has introduced confusion into the world so that we do not always find consistency of moral conduct among men; yet to live in a moral world it is necessary that we put confidence in our fellow man. A complete breakdown of confidence would destroy the adhesive quality of society, tear apart the fabric of civilisation and turn the world into a cage of savage beasts. However bad men may at times become they must still trust each other. It is either confidence or chaos.

What has all this to do with faith in God? Just this: God is a being of supreme moral excellence, possessing in infinite perfection all the qualities that constitute holy character. He deserves and invites the unreserved confidence of every moral creature, including man. Any proper relation to Him must be by confidence, that is, by faith. Where there is no faith it is impossible to please God.

Human sin began with loss of faith in God. When our mother Eve listened to Satan's sly innuendoes against the character of God she began to entertain a doubt of His integrity and right there the doors were opened to the incoming of every possible evil, and darkness settled upon the world.

The Bible talks about man's being alienated from an enemy to God. Should this sound harsh or extreme you have only to imagine your closest personal friend coming to you and stating in cold seriousness that he no longer has any confidence in you. 'I do not trust you. I have lost confidence in your character. I am forced to suspect every move you make.' Such a declaration would instantly alienate friends by destroying the foundation upon which every friendship is built. Until your former friend's opinion of you had been reversed there could be no further communion. Only a restored faith could bring about a restored friendship.

Now, it is well known that people do not go boldly to God and profess that they have no confidence in Him, and no one except the rare professional unbeliever is willing to witness publicly to his low view of God. The frightful thing, however, is that people everywhere act out their unbelief with a consistency that is more convincing than words.

Idolatry is the supreme sin and unbelief is the child of idolatry. Both are libels on the character of the Most High and the Most Holy. 'He that believeth not God hath made him a liar,' wrote the apostle John. A God who lies is a God without character, and where there is no character there can be no confidence. This is the moral logic of unbelief. The unbeliever refuses to trust God because his conception of God is base and ignoble. That he does not burn incense to a graven image does not make him less an idolater, unless we want to make a distinction and say that the idolater worships his false god while the unbeliever refuses to do even that.

The joyous message of Christianity is that there is a

way back from this place of unbelief and alienation. 'He that cometh to God must believe that he is, and that he is a rewarder of them that diligently seek him.' The gospel message declares that the wronged God took the wrong upon Himself in order that the one who committed the wrong might be saved.

Repentance is among other things a sincere apology to God for distrusting Him so long, and faith is throwing oneself upon Christ in complete confidence. Thus by faith reconciliation is achieved between God and man.

33

The Bed of Procrustes

Legend tells of Procrustes, the Greek bandit, who forced his victims to lie on a certain bed. If they were shorter than the bed they were stretched to bed length; if too long they were lopped off to fit. Old Procrustes *would* have uniformity, regardless.

Our modern passion for uniformity has strapped us all to the bed of Procrustes. Our houses, our cars, our clothes are all trimmed to a pattern arbitrarily fixed by persons who have no more right to decide such a thing than Procrustes had to decide how tall a man should be.

It is in the fields of education and religion that the longing for uniformity has done the greatest harm. The effort to standardise people ignores one important fact, viz., that people are not all alike. The idea of equality among all men is totally unrealistic, and any effort to make them all alike contradicts plain evidence, flies in the face of nature and interferes with human freedom.

Equality of opportunity should be granted to all; after that everyone is on his own. No institution can add to or take from the original human stuff the student brings to class with him. After years of observation I am forced to conclude that some persons simply cannot profit from their educational opportunities. Beyond providing them with a few items of information they might not otherwise acquire, a college course does them little good. Their years of enforced study leave them without improved tastes, without perspective and without wisdom. Some persons can gain a good education from life; others cannot manage to become educated by life plus long years in the best institutions of higher learning. Yet our educators continue to apply their Procrustean rules to each new generation, stretching and cutting till they achieve a uniformity Mother Nature obviously never intended.

In the field of religion things are no better. Within the holy precincts of the church Procrustes works on, cutting and tugging till everyone looks, thinks and acts like everyone else. To achieve this he must destroy our originality, make us afraid to be different and persuade us that conformity is synonymous with godliness and nonconformity a sin. And this he does with astonishing success.

Experience proves that uniformity almost always degenerates into mediocrity. It is easier to go down to the contented many than to rise above them; it is easier to memorise than to think through; it is easier to imitate than to initiate. For this reason fundamentalism has over the last half century lost its glow and its wonder and become a dry and tasteless thing from which countless God-hungry persons are turning reluctantly away.

It is unfortunate that current Christianity appears to offer but two choices: dull, colourless orthodoxy or a liberalism which, in its effort to escape suffocation, has jumped overboard and drowned in the maelstrom of unbelief. Actually we are not shut up to any such choices.

God has given us a broad world of truth for our spiritual and intellectual habitation. This universe of truth is to the human soul as limitless as the air to a bird or the sea to a fish. There the Christian mind can luxuriate at perfect liberty. While the ages unfold the believer will need no more than has been already given, for it represents the broad and manifold will of God, the happy home of saints and angels.

This vast sea of truth is expressed in nature, in the Holy Scriptures and in Christ, the Wisdom of God incarnate. Its rational phase can be reduced to a creed which may be learned as one would learn any other truth, and which when so learned constitutes Christian orthodoxy, best and most perfectly embodied in the beliefs of modern evangelical Christianity.

But we must also remember that orthodoxy is not synonymous with Procrustean uniformity. We may bring every thought into accord with divine revelation without sacrificing our intellectual freedom. We can be orthodox without becoming mentally stultified. We can believe every tenet of the Christian creed and still leave our imagination free to roam at will through the broad worlds of nature and grace. We are free but not 'free thinkers'.

The difference between the 'free thinker' and the Christian thinker is that the Christian has faith, and faith is an extra organ of knowledge which the other refuses to acknowledge. The Christian begins where the unbeliever ends, or at least where he hopes to end. The Christian has a fixed ramp from which to take off while the man of no faith must rise from a movable base. The Christian's flights of thought are within the proper world where God has placed him; the unbeliever soon flutters out of the world of assured truth into a misty region of shadow where he can be sure of nothing.

Christ is the light of the world, and His presence illuminates not only the spirits but the minds of His people. As star differs from star in glory, so the children of God are different one from another. They are alike in being members of Christ's Body, but as different as bodily members must of necessity be. To impose upon them an artificial uniformity is to do them great harm.

34

Importance of the
Devotional Mood

Maintenance of the devotional mood is indispensable to success in the Christian life.

Holiness and power are not qualities that can be once received and thereafter forgotten as one might wind a clock or take a vitamin pill. The world is too much with us, not to mention the flesh and the devil, and every advance in the spiritual life must be made against the determined resistance of this trinity of evil. Gains made must be consolidated and held with a resolution equal to that of an army in the field.

To establish our hearts in the devotional mood we must abide in Christ, walk in the Spirit, pray without ceasing and meditate on the Word of God day and night. Of course this implies separation from the world, renunciation of the flesh and obedience to the will of God as we are able to understand it.

And what is the devotional mood? It is nothing else than constant awareness of God's enfolding presence, the holding of inward conversations with Christ and private worship of God in spirit and in truth. Public worship embraces the community of believers and is genuine only as the individuals who compose the company assemble in the mood of reverent devotion. Anything short of this is sheer formality and must surely be unacceptable to God.

Among the enemies to devotion none is so harmful as distractions. Whatever excites the curiosity, scatters the thoughts, disquiets the heart, absorbs the interests or shifts our life focus from the kingdom of God within us to the world around us – that is a distraction; and the world is full of them. Our science-based civilisation has given us many benefits but it has multiplied our distractions and so taken away far more than it has given.

One thing is certain, however: we cannot turn the clock back to quieter times, neither can we hide from the persistent clamour of the twentieth century. We must learn to live in such a world as this and be victorious over it.

In the normal course of things a certain number of distractions are bound to come to each one of us; but if we learn to be inwardly still these can be rendered relatively harmless. It would not be hard to compile a long list of names of Christians who carried upon their shoulders the burden of state or the responsiblities of business and yet managed to live in great inward peace with the face of the Lord in full view. They have left us a precious legacy in the form of letters, journals, hymns and devotional books that witness to the ability of Christ to calm the troubled waters of the soul as He once calmed the waves on the Sea of Galilee. And today as always those who listen can hear His still, small voice above the earthquake and the whirlwind.

While the grace of God will enable us to overcome inevitable distractions, we dare not presume upon God's aid and throw ourselves open to unnecessary ones. The roving imagination, an inquisitive interest in other people's business, preoccupation with external affairs beyond what is absolutely necessary: these are certain to lead us into serious trouble sooner or later. The heart is like a garden and must be kept free from weeds and insects. To expect the fruits and flowers of paradise to grow in an untended heart is to misunderstand completely the processes of grace and the ways of God with men. Only grief and disappointment can result from continued violation of the divine principles that underlie the spiritual life.

The multiplying of artificial objects of attention has not made people happy; it has made them quite the opposite. Think of the contented grandmother, a look of sweet serenity on her face, quietly knitting, and compare her with the nervous exhausted housewife of today, moving tensely among her labour-saving devices trying to get her work finished in time to keep an appointment with her psychiatrist. These pictures may be slightly overdrawn; the grandmother being, possibly, not *quite* so contented and the modern housewife not as frustrated as we suppose, but there is a lot of truth here nevertheless. Things cannot bring happiness; they can only add more weight to the already overburdened heart.

The remedy for distractions is the same now as it was in earlier and simpler times, viz., prayer, meditation and the cultivation of the inner life. The psalmist said 'Be still, and know', and Christ told us to enter into our closet, shut the door and pray unto the Father. It still works.

'Let us return to ourselves, brothers,' said the Greek saint Nicephorus, '...for it is impossible for us to become reconciled and united with God if we do not first return to ourselves, as far as it lies in our power, or if we do not enter within ourselves, tearing ourselves – what a wonder it is! – from the whirl of the world with its multitudinous vain cares and striving constantly to keep attention on the kingdom of heaven which is within us.'

Distractions *must* be conquered or they will conquer

us. So let us cultivate simplicity; let us want fewer things; let us walk in the Spirit; let us fill our minds with the Word of God and our hearts with praise. In that way we can live in peace even in such a distraught world as this. 'Peace I leave with you, my peace I give unto you.'

35

Christian! Love Not the World

The New Testament teaches that to be a follower of Christ it is necessary that a man turn his back upon the world and have no fellowship with it.

Our Lord drew a sharp line between the kingdom of God and the world and said that no one could be at the same time a lover of both. This was also the teaching of Paul, James and John (2 Corinthians 6:14–18; James 4:4; 1 John 2:15–17). It is therefore of critical importance that we who claim to be disciples of Christ should check our relation to the world.

The question of the Christian and the world is not, however, as simple as it might seem. There is much difference of opinion among Christians as to what constitutes the world. Before we can be sure of our relation to something we must first know what it is.

The fact is that two worlds coexist around us. One God made out of nothing; the other man made by taking the materials that originally came from God and fashioning them into a moral caricature of the original.

Both these worlds have been affected by the Fall but only one has been interdicted by the command of God. The non-moral, non-intelligent creation usually called 'nature' has been injured by the spiritual collapse of man, the being for whom it was created, yet because it is non-personal it cannot be evil. We are not forbidden to love the world of nature provided we understand it to be the gift of God and do not confuse it with God Himself, as some have done.

When the Lord brought the children of Israel out of Egypt, where they had been for four hundred years subjected to at least the sight of idolatry, He warned them against the worship of nature. 'Take ye therefore good heed unto yourselves...lest thou lift up thine eyes unto heaven, and when thou seest the sun, and the moon, and the stars, even all the host of heaven, shouldest be driven to worship them, and serve them, which the Lord thy God hath divided unto all nations under the whole heaven' (Deuteronomy 4:15–19).

To persons brought up in the Judaeo-Christian tradition the thought that anyone should actually worship nature seems absurd, but we have only to step across into almost any of the cultures we call pagan to learn that such worship has been and still is common enough. Indeed there is scarcely a natural object anywhere that has not been worshipped by someone.

The created world is to be prized for its usefulness, loved for its beauty and esteemed as the gift of God to His children. Love of natural beauty which has been the source of so much pure music, poetry and art is a good and desirable thing. Though the unregenerate soul is likely to enjoy nature for its own sake and ignore the God whose gift it is, there is nothing to prevent an enlightened Christian who loves God supremely from loving all things for God's dear sake. This would appear to be altogether in accord with the spirit of the psalms and the prophets, and though there is less emphasis upon nature in the New Testament much appreciation of natural things may be found there also.

What, then, is that world against which we are warned by the apostles? That world whose friendship constitutes spiritual adultery, the love of which stands in opposition to the love of God?

It is the familiar world of sinful human society which swells about and beneath us as the waters of the flood once surged and churned around the ark of Noah. No Christian need fail to recognise it, provided he *wants* to know what it is and where it is located. Here are a few infallible marks of identification:

1. *Unbelief.* Wherever men refuse to come under the authority of the inspired Scriptures, there is the world. Religion without the Son of God is worldly religion. To have fellowship with those who live in unbelief is to love the world. The Christian's communion should be with Christians.

2. *Impenitence.* The people of the world will readily admit that they are sinners, but their lack of sorrow for sin distinguishes them from the children of God. The Christian mourns over his sin and is comforted. The worldling shrugs off his sin and continues in it.

3. *Godless philosophies.* Whether they know it or not, they who belong to the world live by a creed, and by their fruits we may know what their creed is.

The man of the world, despite his protestations to the contrary, actually accepts the sufficiency of this world and makes no provision for any other; he esteems earth above heaven, time above eternity, body above soul and men above God. He holds sin to be relatively harmless, believes pleasure to be an end in itself, accepts the rightness of the customary and trusts to the basic goodness of human nature. And even though he be an elder in a church he is part and parcel of the world.

4. *Externalism.* The man of heaven lives for the kingdom within him; the man of earth lives for the world around him. The first is born of the Spirit; the other is

born of the flesh and will perish with it.

To sum up: whatever promotes self, cheapens life, starves the soul, hopes without biblical grounds for hope, adopts current moral standards, follows the way of the majority whether it be right or wrong, indulges in the pleasures of the flesh to make bearable the secret thoughts of death and judgement – that is the world.

'Love not the world, neither the things that are in the world. If any man love the world, the love of the Father is not in him' (1 John 2:15).

36

Substitutes for Discipleship

In the New Testament salvation and discipleship are so closely related as to be indivisible. They are not identical, but as with Siamese twins they are joined by a tie which can be severed only at the price of death.

Yet they *are* being severed in evangelical circles today. In the working creed of the average Christian salvation is held to be immediate and automatic, while discipleship is thought to be something optional which the Christian may delay indefinitely or never accept at all.

It is not uncommon to hear Christian workers urging seekers to accept Christ now and leave moral and social questions to be decided later. The notion is that obedience and discipleship are unrelated to salvation. We may be saved by believing a historic fact about Jesus Christ (that He died for our sins and rose again) and applying this to our personal situation. The whole biblical concept of lordship and obedience is completely absent from the mind of the seeker. He needs help, and Christ is the very one, even the only one, who can furnish it, so he 'takes' Him as his personal Saviour. The idea of His lordship is completely ignored.

The absence of the concept of discipleship from present-day Christianity leaves a vacuum which we instinctively try to fill with one or another substitute. I name a few.

1. *Pietism*. By this I mean an enjoyable feeling of affection for the person of our Lord which is valued for itself and is wholly unrelated to cross-bearing or the keeping of the commandments of Christ.

It is entirely possible to feel for Jesus an ardent love which is not of the Holy Spirit. Witness the love for the Virgin felt by certain devout souls, a love which in the very nature of things must be purely subjective. The heart is adept at emotional tricks and is entirely capable of falling in love with imaginary objects or romantic religious ideas.

In the confused world of romance young persons are constantly inquiring how they can tell when they are 'in love'. They are afraid they may mistake some other sensation for true love and are seeking some trustworthy criterion by which they can judge the quality of their latest emotional fever. Their confusion of course arises from the erroneous notion that love is an enjoyable inward passion, without intellectual or volitional qualities and carrying with it no moral obligations.

Our Lord gave us a rule by which we can test our love for Him: 'He that hath my commandments, and keepeth them, he it is that loveth me: and he that loveth me shall be loved of my Father, and I will love him, and will manifest myself to him.... If a man love me, he will keep my words.... He that loveth me not keepeth not my sayings' (John 14:21–24).

These words are too plain to need much interpreting. Proof of love for Christ is simply removed altogether from the realm of the feelings and placed in the realm of practical obedience. I think the rest of the New Testament is in full accord with this.

2. Another substitute for discipleship is *literalism*. Our Lord referred to this when He reproached the Pharisees for their habit of tithing mint and anise and cumin while at the same time omitting the weightier matters of the law such as justice, mercy and faith. Literalism manifests itself among us in many ways, but it can always be identified in that it lives by the letter of the Word while ignoring its spirit. It habitually fails to apprehend the inward meaning of Christ's words, and contents itself with external compliance with the text. If Christ commands baptism, for instance, it finds fulfillment in the act of water baptism, but the radical meaning of the act as explained in Romans 6 is completely overlooked. It reads the Scriptures regularly, contributes consistently to religious work, attends church every Sunday and otherwise carries on the common duties of a Christian: and for this it is to be commended. Its tragic breakdown is its failure to comprehend the lordship of Christ in the believer's discipleship, separation from the world and the crucifixion of the natural man.

Literalism attempts to build a holy temple upon the sandy foundation of the religious self. It will suffer, sacrifice, and labour, but it will not die. It is Adam at his pious best, but it has never denied self to take up the cross and follow Christ.

3. Another substitute for discipleship I would mention (though these do not exhaust the list) is *zealous religious activity*.

Working for Christ has today been accepted as the ultimate test of godliness among all but a few evangelical Christians. Christ has become a project to be promoted or a cause to be served instead of a Lord to be obeyed. Thousands of mistaken persons seek to do for Christ whatever their fancy suggests should be done, and in whatever way they think best. The *what* and the *how* of Christian service can only originate in the sovereign will of our Lord, but the busy beavers among us ignore this fact and think up their own schemes. The result is an army of men who will run without being sent and speak without being commanded.

To avoid the snare of unauthorised substitution I recommend a careful and prayerful study of the lordship of Christ and the discipleship of the believer.

37

The Marks of God's Chosen

The Christian Scriptures, particularly the Gospel of John, contain two truths which appear to stand opposed to each other.

One is that whosoever will may come to Christ. The other is that before anyone can come there must have been a previous work done in his heart by the sovereign operation of God.

The notion that just anybody, at any time, regardless of conditions, can start from religious scratch, without the Spirit's help, and believe savingly on Christ by a sudden decision of the will, is wholly contrary to the teachings of the Bible.

God's invitation to men is broad but not unqualified. The word 'whosoever' throws the door open wide, indeed, but the Church in recent years has carried the gospel invitation far beyond its proper bounds and turned it into something more human and less divine than that found in the sacred Scriptures.

What we tend to overlook is that the word 'whosoever' never stands by itself. Always its meaning is modified by the word 'believe' or 'will' or 'come'. According to the teachings of Christ no man will or can come and believe unless there has been done within him a prevenient work of God enabling him so to do.

In the sixth chapter of John our Lord makes some statements which gospel Christians seem afraid to talk about. The average one of us manages to live with them by the simple trick of ignoring them. They are such as these: 1. Only they come to Christ who have been given to Him by the Father (John 6:37). 2. No one can come of himself; he must first be drawn by the Father (John 6:44). 3. The ability to come to Christ is a gift of the Father (John 6:65). 4. Everyone given to the Son by the Father will come to Him (John 6:37).

It is not surprising that upon hearing these words many of our Lord's disciples went back and walked no more with Him. Such teaching cannot but be deeply disturbing to the natural mind. It takes from sinful men much of the power of self-determination upon which they had prided themselves so inordinately. It cuts the ground out from under their self-help and throws them back upon the sovereign good pleasure of God, and that is precisely where they do not want to be. They are willing to be saved by grace, but to preserve their self-esteem they must hold that the desire to be saved originated with them; this desire is their contribution to the whole thing, their offering of the fruit of the ground, and it keeps salvation in their hands where in truth it is not and never can be.

Admitting the difficulties this creates for us, and acknowledging that it runs contrary to the assumptions of popular Christianity, it is yet impossible to deny that there are certain persons who, though still unconverted, are nevertheless different from the crowd, marked out of God, stricken with an interior wound and susceptible to the call of Christ to a degree others are not.

About the teaching as a mere doctrine I am not much concerned, but I am keenly interested in learning how to identify such persons. No man is ever the same after God has laid His hand upon him. He will have certain marks, and though they are not easy to detect perhaps we may cautiously name a few.

One mark is *a deep reverence* for divine things. A sense of the sacred must be present or there can be receptivity to God and truth. This mysterious feeling of awe precedes repentance and faith and is nothing else but a gift from heaven. Millions go through life unaffected by the presence of God in His world. Good they may be and honest, but they are nevertheless men of earth, 'finished and finite clods', and proof against every call of the Spirit.

Another mark is *a great moral sensitivity*. Most persons are apathetic, insensitive to matters of the heart and the conscience, and so are not salvable, at least not in their present condition. But when God begins to work in a man to bring him to salvation He makes him acutely sensitive to evil. Inward repulsion toward the swine pen that rouses the prodigal and starts him back home is a gift of God to His chosen.

Another mark of the Spirit's working is *a mighty moral discontent*. In spite of our effort to make sinners think they are unhappy the fact is that wherever social and health conditions permit the masses of mankind enjoy themselves very much. Sin has its pleasures (Hebrews 11:25) and the vast majority of human beings have a whale of a time living. The conscience is a bit of a pest but most persons manage to strike a truce with it quite early in life and are not troubled much by it thereafter.

It takes a work of God in a man to sour him on the world and to turn him against himself; yet until this has happened to him he is psychologically unable to repent and believe. Any degree of contentment with the world's moral standards or his own lack of holiness successfully blocks off the flow of faith into the man's heart. Esau's fatal flaw was moral complacency; Jacob's only virtue was his bitter discontent.

Again before a man can be saved he must feel *a consuming spiritual hunger*. Anyone who lives close to the hearts of men knows that there is little spiritual hunger among them. Religion, pious talk, yes; but not real hunger. Where a hungry heart is found we may be sure that God was there first. 'Ye have not chosen me, but I have chosen you...' (John 15:16).

38

The Passing of the Assembly Concept from Christianity

The Church as announced by Christ, seen in the book of Acts and explained by Paul is a thing of great simplicity and rare beauty.

The Church as we see it today is unsymmetrical, highly complex and anything but beautiful. Indeed I think that if some angel of God were made familiar with the Church as it appears in the New Testament and then sent to the earth to try to locate it, it would be extremely doubtful whether the heavenly messenger would recognise anything now existing in the field of religion as the Church he was looking for. So far have we departed from the pattern shown us in the mount.

The Church as the New Testament pictures it is any company of regenerate believers met in the name of Jesus Christ. Such a company is called out from the world and gathered to Christ as a flock of sheep is gathered to the shepherd. The members of this company constitute a despised minority group standing in bold moral contradiction to the world. Their witness is Christ: His person, work, office and present position at the right hand of the Majesty in the heavens. They carry His gospel to the world and plead 'Be ye reconciled to God', then they return to their own company to worship, pray, teach and listen to the Word of the Lord as it is expounded by men of God. They also exhort, testify and exercise for the good of all such spiritual gifts as each one may possess from the Spirit.

Every local church is a microcosm, having all the qualities of the macrocosm, the Church universal. Each local company is ideally and should be actually equipped to do anything that the Head of the Church wills to accomplish. Wherever such a company is found, there is the true Church, the complete Church, so complete that if all the believers in the world were to be gathered in one place it would not add anything to the perfection of the smaller assembly.

Each local church is a fellowship in the deepest spiritual meaning of that word. It comes into being by an afflatus of power and a bestowment of life. It cannot be produced by organisation, though after it is there it may be strengthened and improved by a wise and Spirit-led organisation. A true Church existed in Crete before Titus was left there to 'set in order the things that are wanting, and ordain elders in every city'. Organisation did not create the Church; it was imposed upon a Church already present, a Church which had been born out of the preaching of the gospel. For it is always the gospel that produces the Church; there can be no Church apart from the gospel.

Leaving out of consideration other problems and other times we'll look briefly at two forces that have worked to destroy the assembly concept in this generation:

The first is *denominationalism*, the dividing of believing men into mutually exclusive camps. This is not peculiar to these times, but we today are reaping the fruit of a tree planted long ago. Though I have for many years worked in a denomination and preached freely among other denominations I am not blind to the mischief that accompanies this extra scriptural phenomenon.

I do not here offer a remedy for denominationalism. I merely report the facts, and they are not encouraging. To enter any place of worship where the saints of God meet conscious of denominational loyalites or hostilities is to lose completely the sense of communion with Christ and each other so vital to true worship. I believe a few individual saints may be godly enough to escape the trap, but I am sure the larger numbers are not.

Another force that has helped to block out the New Testament concept of the Church is *tabernacleism*. This phenomenon flourished during the second and third decade of this century, and though it has passed it has unfortunately left behind it the religious philosophy that brought it into being, as well as the spirit and mood it created.

Tabernacleism, oddly enough, came as a revolt from denominationalism. Certain gifted men got their fill of ecclesiastical machinery and broke away to start independent religious groups made up of others like themselves. Often with but a modicum of theological knowledge and with no time nor inclination to learn, they turned to the theatre for their technique. And it worked, surprisingly, astonishingly well.

The concept of the Church held by the founders and promoters of *tabernacleism* may be learned easily enough by noticing the nomenclature that accompanied it: 'work' instead of assembly or church; 'programme' instead of worship; 'artist' (used for any fifth-rate performer on the handsaw or consecrated cowbells); 'talent' (to refer to a performer); 'one night appearance', 'in person' (borrowed from the theatre), and many other such terms, unconscious confessions that the saints had left the ways of God and gone in the ways of fallen men. And this while making the strongest protestations of orthodoxy.

I do not mean to scold, and I am grateful for any shreds of New Testament worship that may be left among us; but I cannot but hope and pray that the evangelical church may soon return to the land of promise. We have been in Babylon long enough. And one of the first things she must rediscover before she comes home is her own identity.

39

What the Advent Established

The announcement of the birth of Christ came as a sunburst of joy to a world where grief and pain are known to all and joy comes rarely and never tarries long.

The joy the angel brought to the awe-struck shepherds was not to be a disembodied wisp of religious emotion, swelling and ebbing like the sound of an aeolian harp in the rising and falling of the wind. Rather it was and is a state of lasting gladness resulting from tidings that there was born in the city of David a Saviour which is Christ the Lord. It was an overflowing sense of well-being that had every right to be there.

The birth of Christ told the world something. That He should come to be born of a woman, to make Himself of no reputation and, being found in fashion as a man, to humble Himself even to death on a cross – this is a fact so meaningful, so eloquent as to elude even the power of a David or an Isaiah fully to celebrate. His coming, I repeat, told the world something; it declared something, established something. What was it?

That something was several things, and as Christ broke the loaves into pieces for greater convenience in eating, let me divide the message into parts the easier to understand it. The Advent established:

First, that God is real. The heavens were opened and another world than this came into view. A message came from beyond the familiar world of nature. 'Glory to God in the highest,' chanted the celestial host, 'and on earth peace, good will.' Earth the shepherds know too well; now they hear from God and heaven above. Our earthly world and the world above blend into one scene and in joyous excitement the shepherds can but imperfectly distinguish the one from the other.

It is little wonder that they went in haste to see Him who had come from above. To them God was no longer a hope, a desire that He might be. He was real.

Second, human life is essentially spiritual. With the emergence into human flesh of the Eternal Word of the Father the fact of man's divine origin is confirmed. God could not incarnate Himself in a being wholly flesh or even essentially flesh. For God and man to unite they must be to some degree like each other. It had to be so.

The Incarnation may indeed raise some questions, but it answers many more. The ones it raises are speculative; the ones it settles are deeply moral and vastly important to the souls of men. Man's creation in the image and likeness of God is one question it settles by affirming it positively. The advent proves it to be a literal fact.

Third, God indeed spoke by the prophets. The priests and scribes who were versed in the Scriptures could inform the troubled Herod that the Christ was to be born in Bethlehem of Judaea. And thereafter the Old Testament came alive in Christ. It was as if Moses and David and Isaiah and Jeremiah and all the minor prophets hovered around Him, guiding His footsteps into the way of the prophetic Scriptures.

So difficult was the Old Testament gamut the Messiah must run to validate His claims that the possiblity of anyone's being able to do it seemed utterly remote; yet

Jesus did it, as a comparison of the Old Testament with the New will demonstrate. His coming confirmed the veracity of the Old Testament Scriptures, even as those Scriptures confirmed the soundness of His own claims.

Fourth, man is lost but not abandoned. The coming of Christ to the world tells us both of these things.

Had men not been lost no Saviour would have been required. Had they been abandoned no Saviour would have come. But He came, and it is now established that God has a concern for men. Though we have sinned away every shred of merit, still He has not forsaken us. 'For the Son of man is come to seek and to save that which was lost.'

Fifth, the human race will not be exterminated. That which was God seized upon that which was man. 'God of the substance of His Father, begotten before all ages; Man of the substance of His mother, born in the world. Perfect God and perfect Man…who, although He be God and man, yet He is not two but one Christ.' God did not visit the race to rescue it; in Christ He took human nature unto Himself, and now He is one of us.

For this reason we may be certain that mankind will not be wiped out by a nuclear explosion or turned into subhuman monsters by the effects of radiation on the human genetic processes. Christ did not take upon Himself the nature of a race soon to be extinct.

Sixth, this world is not the end. Christ spoke with cheerful certainty of the world to come. He reported on things He had seen and heard in heaven and told of the many mansions awaiting us. We are made for two worlds and as surely as we now inhabit the one we shall also inhabit the other.

Seventh, death will some day be abolished and life and immortality hold sway. 'For this purpose the Son of God was manifested, that he might destroy the works of the devil,' and what more terrible work has the devil accomplished than to bring sin to the world and death by sin? But life is now made manifest by the appearing of our Saviour Jesus Christ, who hath abolished death and hath brought life and immortality to light through the gospel.

40

Quality Versus Quantity in Religion

The emphasis today in Christian circles appears to be on quantity, with a corresponding lack of emphasis on quality. Numbers, size and amount seem to be very nearly all that matters even among evangelicals. The size of the crowd, the number of converts, the size of the budget, the amount of weekly collections: if these look good the church is prospering and the pastor is thought to be a success. The church that can show an impressive quantitative growth is frankly envied and imitated by other ambitious churches.

This is the age of the Laodiceans. The great goddess *Numbers* is worshipped with fervent devotion and all things religious are brought before her for examination. Her Old Testament is the financial report and her New Testament is the membership roll. To these she appeals as arbiters of all questions, the test of spiritual growth and the proof of success or failure in every Christian endeavour.

A little acquaintance with the Bible should show this up for the heresy it is. To judge anything spiritual by statistics is to judge by another than scriptural judgement. It is to admit the validity of externalism and to deny the value our Lord places upon the soul as over against the body. It is to mistake the old creation for the new and to confuse things eternal with things temporal. Yet it is being done every day by ministers, church boards and denominational leaders. And hardly anyone notices the deep and dangerous error.

Our most pressing obligation today is to do all in our power to obtain a revival that will result in a reformed, revitalised, purified church. It is of far greater importance that we have better Christians than that we have more of them. Each generation of Christians is the seed of the next, and degenerate seed is sure to produce a degenerate harvest not a little better than but a little worse than the seed from which it sprang. Thus the direction will be down until vigorous, effective means are taken to improve the seed.

And how can we improve the church? Simply and only by improving ourselves: and there is where the difficulty lies. The church in any locality is what its individual members are, no better and no worse. We as members must begin by seeking moral amendment that will result in a positive spiritual renaissance. And that is why improvement is hard to achieve. As long as we can keep the whole thing at arm's length and deal with it academically we may preach and write about it at little or no real cost to ourselves and, it must be admitted, with no real advance in godliness.

If we would be followers of Christ indeed we must become personally and vitally involved in His death and resurrection. And this requires repentance, prayer, watchfulness, self-denial, detachment from the world, humility, obedience and cross carrying. That is why it is easier to talk about revival than to experience it.

To avoid personal involvement with the cross we have

become adept at finding or creating religious projects to soothe our conscience and make things look good. Among these may be named evangelism and foreign missions. These are good, scriptural activities, incumbent upon all Christians, but all pre-suppose that they who engage in them should be holy, Spirit-filled and totally committed to God. To carry on these activities scripturally the church should be walking in fullness of power, separated, purified and ready at any moment to give up everything, even life itself, for the greater glory of Christ. For a worldly, weak, decadent church to make converts is but to bring forth after her own kind and extend her weakness and decadence a bit further out.

A farmer sows wheat and, granted that the soil is fertile, his harvest will be only what the seed was, allowing for the slight natural retrogression that usually follows each careless planting. Is it not plain that the quality of the seed is what matters most? Would it not be folly for the farmer to grow more and more and poorer and poorer wheat? Let him look to his seed if he would improve his harvest.

Should someone object that the seed is the Word and that since the Word remains always the same it will produce the same effect wherever and by whomsoever it is preached, I would reply that the first is true but not the second. Verily God's Word is ever the same, but what it will do at any time in any place depends largely upon the moral purity, wisdom and spiritual power of those who preach it. There is nothing automatic about the truth. To do its most effective work it must be incarnated in the church.

Look at Acts 18 and 19. Apollos, a man mighty in the Scriptures, for all his faithfulness to the truth as he understood it, could produce only imperfect converts. Suppose Paul had not arrived when he did. It is not hard to imagine an immature, weak and ineffective church propagating itself in Ephesus.

So vitally important is spiritual quality that it is hardly too much to suggest that attempts to grow larger might well be suspended until we have become better.

41

The Honest Use of
Religious Words

A disturbing phenomenon of the day is the new and tricky use of familiar words.

A 'people's republic', for instance, is not a republic nor does it belong to the people. The word 'freedom' now in most countries refers to something so restricted that a generation or two ago another word altogether would have been chosen to describe it.

Other words that have changed their meanings without admitting it are 'war', 'peace', 'grant' (to describe the small sop the government tosses back out of the money it has previously taken from us), 'right', 'left', 'equality', 'security', 'liberal' and many more. These have been emptied of their meaning and a different meaning has been poured into them. We may now read them or hear them spoken and, unless we are very sharp, gain from them a wholly false idea.

This phenomenon has invaded the field of religion also. In a predominantly Christian society such as prevails in the West the words of Scripture and of Christian theology have quite naturally acquired a fixed meaning and until recently always meant the same thing whenever they were used by educated and responsible persons. With the coming of the various revolutions – scientific, industrial, philosophical, social, artistic, political – fixed meanings have deserted religious words and now float about like disembodied spirits, looking for but apparently never finding the bodies from which they have been exorcised by the revolutionists.

Among religious words which have lost their Christian meaning are 'inspiration', 'revelation', 'spiritual', 'fellowship', 'brotherhood', 'unity', 'worship', 'prayer', 'heaven', 'immortality', 'hell', 'Lord', 'new birth', 'converted' – but the list is long and includes almost every major word of the Christian faith.

Of course I do not refer here to the translation of a word from one language to another, nor to the slow evolution that takes place in the forms of words over the years. I refer to the deliberate use of old and familiar words with fixed meanings in a way that violates those meanings and makes the words convey ideas other than those the hearer has every right to expect. The speaker may employ an orthodox word but he does not mean what the hearer thinks he means, so the hearer is deceived. This is a dishonest use of words.

This trick is reprehensible anywhere, but when used deliberately in the sphere of religion it is no less than an act of sheer moral turpitude.

The constant use of biblical terms to express non-biblical concepts is now common. Yet not everyone who misuses religious words is guilty of wrong intent. For two full generations the habit of emptying words of one meaning and refilling them with another has been taking place among the churches; so it is quite natural that many sincere ministers should engage in theological double talk without knowing it.

Certain biblical words along with certain theological terms embody what God has given to be intellectually grasped by man. It is critically important that the same word should mean the same thing to everyone in a given language group. To permit a change in meaning is to invite disaster. To preserve life the physician and the druggist use words of fixed meaning common to both. How much more should the pulpit and the pew have a clear understanding about the words of eternal life.

The modern effort to popularise the Christian faith has been extremely damaging to that faith. The purpose has been to simplify truth for the masses by using the language of the masses instead of the language of the church. It has not succeeded, but has added to rather than diminished religious confusion.

Positive beliefs are not popular these days. A mistaken desire to maintain a spirit of tolerance among all races and religions has produced a breed of Janus-like Christians with built-in swivels, remarkable only for their ability to turn in any direction gracefully. The philosophy behind this whole thing is that religious beliefs are matters of personal choice, and that the Lord adapts His saving truth to the individual, varying it according to the cultural background, educational level and social situation of each one. Whatever this is, it is not Christianity.

A number of popular religious books have appeared of late quite literally filled with swivel-words of uncertain meaning; and because these were written by persons ostensibly evangelical they have been accepted and promoted by the evangelicals. And they are having a real influence on Christian thinking; or more to the point, they are making sound Christian thinking impossible for those who read and admire them. We had better take a good hard look at these books. If the authors will not stand still to let their meanings be examined, there is probably a good reason. Great ideas have a habit of inhabiting the same great words generation after generation. To ignore or reject the word is to reject the idea.

The hope of the church yet lies in the purity of her

theology, that is, her beliefs about God and man and their relation to each other. These beliefs have been revealed to her by the inspiration of the Holy Spirit in the sacred Scriptures. Everything there is clear-cut and accurate. We dare not be less than accurate in our treatment of anything so precious.

42

The Right Attitude toward Our Spiritual Leaders

We have and will always have spiritual leaders.

Even the most democratic-minded Christian is being influenced, and so led to some degree, by some other Christian living or dead. He cannot escape it; that is the way he is made and he might as well accept it.

At the extreme ends of the religious spectrum are those churches that are controlled from the top by an all-powerful heirarchy and those churches that boldly reject any such supreme authority and insist upon complete autonomy within the local assembly. Yet both kinds of churches are controlled by their leaders. The one group admits it, the other denies it; but the control exists for both nevertheless. Admittedly the degree of control is less in the second instance than in the first, but it is there.

That our religious outlook is largely determined for us by our leaders cannot be denied, but whether that is a good or an evil will depend altogether upon the kind of leaders we have and the wisdom we exercise in our attitude toward them.

I think we make two mistakes in our attitude toward

our Christian leaders, one in not being sufficiently grateful to them and the other in following them too slavishly.

The first is a sin of omission, and because it is something that is not there it is not so likely to be noticed as a sin that is plainly present. For instance, it is a sin to be ungrateful to a man who has befriended us, but it is not as bad or as obvious a sin as stealing his pocket-book.

To be grateful to God's servants is to be grateful to God. The benefits we receive from them result from God's working through them, but as free agents they could have refused to cooperate. That they cheerfully yielded their members to the Spirit for our good puts us under continual obligation to them. Because they are so many, and because the vast majority of them have long fallen asleep we cannot make a like return to them in person; the only way we can discharge our obligation is to be thankful. Gratitude is an offering precious in the sight of God, and it is one that the poorest of us can make and be not poorer but richer for having made it.

In a very real sense we thank God when we thank His people. Gratitude felt and expressed becomes a healing, life-building force in the soul. Something wonderful happens within us when gratitude enters. We cannot be too grateful, for it would be like loving too much or being too kind. And if we are to make a mistake it had better be on the side of humble gratitude for benefits received. Should we in error give credit to someone who does not deserve it we are far better off than if we fail to give credit to one who does.

To those holy men who gave us the sacred Scriptures we owe a debt we can never hope to pay. We should be glad they were in such a spiritual state that they could hear the Voice at the critical moment when God would use them to transmit His mighty words to mankind. And to all who in olden times lovingly transcribed the Word, we should be thankful, and to the old saints who at

various dangerous times in the past risked their lives to
preserve the Holy Scriptures inviolate.

There is a common debt that every Christian owes to
his fellow Christians; but there is a heavier debt that he
owes to particular Christians: to Bible scholars, to trans-
lators, to reformers, missionaries, evangelists,
revivalists, hymn writers, composers, pastors, teachers
and praying saints. For these we should keep the incense
of our grateful prayers rising day and night to the Father
of light who is the source and fountain of all our blessings.

If it is a sin of omission to be ungrateful toward our
God-ordained leaders and benefactors it is as surely a sin
to be too dependent upon them. Those men who were
honoured of God to write down the words of the inspired
Scriptures hold a unique position in the providence of
God and we except them from what follows. We are
completely dependent upon the Scriptures for divine
truth and in that sense we must follow the words of the
inspired writers without question. But no other man
holds such a power over us.

We make a serious mistake when we become so
attached to the preaching or writing of a great Christian
leader that we accept his teaching without daring to
examine it. No man is that important in the kingdom of
God. We should follow men only as they follow the Lord
and we should keep an open mind lest we become blind
followers of a man whose breath is in his nostrils.

No Christian leader but has his blind spot, his unconscious prejudices, and these will influence his teachings.
We will have plenty of our own without weakly accept-
ing those of our teachers.

What then shall we do? Learn from every holy man
who exercises a ministry toward us, be grateful to every
one of them and thankful for all, and then follow Christ.
No free believer should ever sell his freedom to another.
No Christian is worthy to be the master of other Chris-

tians. Christ alone is worthy to be called Master; there is no other.

'But the anointing which ye have received of him abideth in you, and ye need not that any man teach you: but as the same anointing teacheth you of all things, and is truth, and is no lie, and even as it hath taught you, ye shall abide in him' (1 John 2:27).

43

The Proper Use of
the Bible

The boast that the Bible is the world's best seller sounds
a little hollow when the character and purpose of the
Bible are understood.

It is not how many Bibles are sold that counts, nor
even how many people read them; what matters is how
many actually believe what they read and surrender
themselves in faith to live by the truth. Short of this the
Bible can have no real value for any of us.

A great deal is said, and rightly said, about the superi-
ority of the Bible as literature. So beautiful are the words
of prophet and psalmist, as well as those of our Lord and
His apostles, that they can scarcely be made less than
beautiful, even by the clumsiest translator. Speaking any
word here in praise of the beauty of the Authorised
Version (the one usually selected to be 'read as literature') would be to gild the lily or set a candle to the sun,
so I refrain. But to study the Scriptures for their literary
beauty alone is to miss the whole purpose for which they
were written.

The Bible was called forth by the moral emergency
occasioned by the fall of man. It is the voice of God
calling men home from the wilds of sin; it is a road map

for returning prodigals; it is instruction in righteousness, light in darkness, information about God and man and life and death and heaven and hell. In it God warns, commands, rebukes, promises, encourages. In it He offers salvation and life through His Eternal Son. And the destiny of each one depends upon the response he or she makes to the voice of the Word.

Because the Bible is the kind of book it is there can be no place for the detached, appraising attitude in our approach to it. 'O earth, earth, earth, hear the word of the Lord.' God's Word is not to be enjoyed as one might enjoy a Beethoven symphony or a poem by Wordsworth. It demands immediate action, faith, surrender, committal. Until it has secured these it has done nothing positive for the reader, but it *has* increased his responsibility and deepened the judgement that must follow.

Of the millions of Bibles bought during the last few years there is no certain way to discover how many are being read. But there is a pretty sure way to discover how many readers obey them. Total committal of a few hundred thousand persons to the message of the Bible anywhere in the world would work a moral revolution that would affect for good every facet of modern life. Since no such revolution has occurred we can only conclude that the best seller is not being read, or at least not being obeyed.

In a time of disaster such as earthquake or flood, first-aid information and the instructions of the medical authorities are often matters of life or death. What would we think of a man if we found him at such a time comfortably reclined reading this material for its literary beauty? He might feel an aesthetic thrill at the terse, concise language and still die of typhoid, for his life depends not upon his admiration of the words of the official directives but upon his obedience to them.

As preposterous as such conduct would be, yet something like it is practiced constantly in a sphere where the consequences are far more weighty. Men who have but a little while to prepare themselves for the eternal world read the only book that can tell them how – not to learn how, but to enjoy the literary beauty of the book. Only the blindness of heart occasioned by sin would permit men so to do.

In recent years the Bible has been recommended for many other purposes than the one for which it was written. The peace of mind cults, for instance, manage to find in it oil for the troubled waters of the soul; but to make it work they must pick, choose, misunderstand and misapply quite literally to their heart's content. Now, the Bible when read honestly and responsibly does bring peace of mind, but only after it has first brought the heart to a repentance that is often anything but peaceful. When the entire life has been morally transformed and the heart purified from sin, then the seeker can know real and legitimate peace. Any manipulation of the Scriptures to make them speak peace to the natural man is evil and can only lead to ruin.

In the hill country of the American South I once met persons who used certain obscure passages from Ezekiel as an incantation to stop blood after an injury. The Bible has also been made to serve as a textbook for salesmen, and some of us remember that during the Depression of the 1930's some distraught leaders suggested that it might be well to adopt the economics of Joseph in Egypt to help pull us out of the hole.

A few years ago it was fairly popular practice for Bible teachers to claim to find in the Scriptures confirmation of almost every new discovery made by science. Apparently no one noticed that the scientist had to find it before the Bible teacher could, and it never seemed to occur to anyone to wonder why, if it was there in the Bible in such plain sight, it took several thousand years and the help of science before anyone saw it.

Now, I believe that everything in the Bible is true, but to attempt to make it a textbook for science is to misunderstand it completely and tragically. The purpose of the Bible is to bring men to Christ, to make them holy and prepare them for heaven. In this it is unique among books, and it always fulfills its purpose when it is read in faith and obedience.

44

Adjusted: But to What?

A word that is being greatly over-used in modern society is 'adjust'.

I am certainly not the first one to complain about it, but my objection to its over-use is, I believe, on a little higher level, for most persons who register their objections are thinking only about its social effects while I am concerned with its effect in the spiritual realm.

Thinking persons who deplore the present mania for adjustment point out that almost all adjustment is made downward to bring people into harmony with the common and the mediocre, so that society is educated toward a dead level with ordinariness as its ultimate end.

This passion to be mediocre and to make everyone else the same begins with the parent in the home, spreads to the schools and is propagated with missionary zeal by the advertisers. And advertising is the most powerful educational agent extant. Those who write the advertising copy probably do more to determine the way the average person thinks than the school and church combined.

The reasons for this are two. One is that men may flee from the admonitions of parents and the good counsel of the church, but where can anyone hide from the advertiser? He is near to being ubiquitous as anything on earth except gravity.

The second reason the advertiser exercises such incredibly powerful influence is that he has learned to perfection the art of communication. He may be lying, and often is, but he does get his ideas across; and that is more than can be said for the school and the church.

The big problem with Christians is that they come to Christ with their minds already made up on one point, viz., to stay sane they must remain adjusted to society. This notion has been drilled into them from their playpen, and it never occurs to them to question it. There is a norm out there somewhere to which they must conform, and that norm is above criticism. Their success and happiness depend upon how well they adjust to it. And Christianity, though it may add something to it, must never disagree with the main idea.

To be happy, adjust to the social norm. That is the popular notion but it will not hold up under examination. This norm to which we must adjust – where did it come from? What Moses brought it down from what mount? Where are its credentials? From whence its authority?

Since the world insists that I adjust to its beliefs, its moral standards and its practical working philosophies, it should be able to demonstrate that it knows where it is going, what it wants and why, and it should be able to come up with a few million happy men and women who by adjusting to its standards have found life's *summum bonum*. Furthermore, nations that have had the benefit of such adjustment should be prosperous, peaceful, contented and happy.

These stipulations do not appear to me at all unreasonable considering how much depends upon the outcome and how much evangelistic zeal the world puts into the effort to get everyone properly adjusted.

But these simple tests show how phony the whole thing is. The truth is that the world does *not* know where it is going; it has *not* found life's *summum bonum*; it is *not* qualified as a model for the members of society to follow. It is instead puzzled, frightened and frustrated. Generation follows generation into an uncertain future, completely beaten, disappointed and sick at heart.

It was to this kind of world that Jesus came, to save it from itself. He died for its sins and now lives for the salvation of all who will repudiate it, deny the validity of its philosophies and put their trust wholly in the Lord Jesus Christ.

Those who do this no longer seek to be adjusted to society. They have renounced this world and have chosen a new model after which to pattern their lives. This is the aspect of the Christian life that most people do not like. They want comfort, blessing and peace, but they recoil from this radical, revolutionary break with the world. To follow Christ in this rough and thorough-going way is too much for them.

The true Christian, though he is in revolt against the world's efforts to brainwash him, is no mere rebel for rebellion's sake. He dissents from the world because he knows that it cannot make good on its promises. He has tasted the pleasures of society and he knows that they leave a bitter taste; and he has found that blessing of the Lord of which the wise man speaks, which maketh rich and addeth no sorrow with it.

And the Christian is not left without a 'norm' to which he seeks to become adjusted. The Lord Jesus Christ is Himself the norm, the ideally perfect model, and the worshipping soul yearns to be like Him. Indeed the whole drive behind the Christian life is this longing to be conformed to the image of Christ. The energy with which the believing man revolts against conformity to the image of unregenerate society will be in exact proportion to the intensity of his yearning to be like Christ.

The classic expression of this burning desire to be Christlike is, of course, Paul's personal testimony in his letter to the Philippian Christians which begins, 'But what things were gain to me, those I counted loss for Christ,' and ends with the fervent declaration, 'I press toward the mark for the prize of the high calling of God in Christ Jesus' (3:7–14).

Faith Beyond Reason

by A. W. Tozer

A. W. Tozer earned the reputation of 'twentieth century prophet', for he had a close walk with God and recognised the real issues at stake among evangelical Christians.

Here *faith* is the primary issue; Dr Tozer insists upon a faith that soars beyond reason to rest upon the character of God. Other areas covered include the *conscience*, the *transformed nature*, *usefulness in service* and the *second coming of Christ*.

A joint publication

 Kingsway Publications and STL Books